PACIFIC COAST
HIGHWAY
TRAVEL GUIDE
202
BEST STOPS

ROAD TRIP FROM SEATTLE TO SAN DIEGO
SOUTHBOUND EDITION
MARK WATSON

SEATTLE  SAN DIEGO

THIS VERSION OF THE TRAVEL GUIDE
IS FOR PEOPLE TRAVELING
FROM SEATTLE
TO SAN DIEGO
S O U T H B O U N D

PACIFIC COAST HWY

THIS TRAVEL GUIDE BELONGS TO:

....

'LATE AFTERNOON ON THE WEST COAST ENDS WITH THE SKY DOING ALL ITS BRILLIANT STUFF.'

JOAN DIDION

DEDICATED TO ALL PACIFIC COAST HIGHWAY TRAVELERS FROM ALL OVER THE WORLD

TABLE OF CONTENTS

INTRODUCTION

THIS TRAVEL GUIDE WAS CREATED TO HELP YOU EXPLORE THE PACIFIC COAST HIGHWAY BY ANY MODE OF TRANSPORTATION AND HELP YOU HAVE AN UNFORGETTABLE TRAVEL EXPERIENCE. YOU'LL DISCOVER THE TOP 202 DESTINATIONS ALONG THIS SCENIC ROUTE, WITH HELPFUL REMINDERS TO ENSURE YOU DON'T MISS ANY OF THE HIGHLIGHTS!

ARE YOU READY TO START YOUR JOURNEY?

RULES

This travel guide has rules that you must follow to have fun and stay safe:

① This book conveniently lists Pacific Coast Highway destinations in the order that they appear on the road, allowing you to easily explore the area and visit each location.

② Before you start, plan your route. Consider the amount of time you have to travel. Then select the places that seem most interesting to you. If you would like to visit a particular stop during your journey, be sure to mark it as "TO VISIT" at the top left corner of the page.

③ 52 stops out of the 202 included in this travel guide are marked "Iconic Place." Keep a close eye out for those! If you have limited time for your Pacific Coast Highway trip (no more than 7-10 days), I suggest you limit your travel to only these locations. Visiting all the points in this book will take approximately 3-4 weeks.

④ Some places are marked "Off the Main Route." To see them you have to make a slight detour. Remember, since these are not visible from the Pacific Coast Highway, you have to be extra sure not to miss them! If your time is limited for the journey, you can choose which of these attractions to visit and which to skip.

RULES

---

(5) Every time you visit a location, remember to check "VISITED" at the top left corner of the page.

(6) You can navigate to each destination by scanning the QR code with your smartphone, using the included GPS coordinates, or inputting the address into your navigation system of choice. Remember, on some sections of the Pacific Coast Highway you will be offline with no access to cellular data. The best way to navigate in these sections is with a standard GPS unit (i.e. Garmin navigation) by using the GPS coordinates.

(7) Don't forget to complete the travel journal each day. This can be found at the end of the guide.

(8) To make your journey easier, this travel guide includes easy to follow maps.

(9) The destinations were objectively selected by the author as the most interesting. However, do not be afraid to add your own stops if another place catches your interest. The selection of places for this book was not influenced by any financial contributions for promotion.

(10) The travel guide also contains a list of recommended lodgings and RV parks. In addition, speed limits are included. Follow the regulations and speed limits indicated on the road signs.

FREQUENTLY ASKED QUESTIONS

What and where is the Pacific Coast Highway?

The Pacific Coast Highway is a stunningly beautiful and iconic road that stretches along the western edge of the United States. It winds through some of the most scenic and picturesque landscapes in the country, with breathtaking ocean views, rugged cliffs, and majestic mountains. The route is a popular destination for road trippers, tourists, and adventure seekers, and offers a wide range of attractions and activities along the way. Starting from Seattle in the north, the Pacific Coast Highway meanders southwards through the states of Washington, Oregon, and California, before ending in San Diego. If you drive northbound, the Pacific Coast Highway starts in San Diego, California and ends in Seattle, Washington. The road is not officially named the Pacific Coast Highway for its entire length, but is commonly referred to as such due to its proximity to the Pacific Ocean. The road is also known as the Pacific Highway, and consists of several major routes, including Highways 1 and 101.

How long is the Pacific Coast Highway?

Determining the exact length of the PCH is difficult because it is not a single, continuous road, but rather a network of roads that connect various coastal cities and towns. There are several different routes considered part of the Pacific Coast Highway, and each has its own length and unique features. That being said, based on maps and available information, it's estimated that the Pacific Coast Highway from Seattle, WA to San Diego, CA is approximately 1775 miles long. However, this number is subject to change depending on the specific route taken and any detours that may be necessary.

FREQUENTLY ASKED QUESTIONS

What is the difference between Pacific Coast Highway, Route 101 and California Highway 1?

Pacific Coast Highway (PCH), Route 101, and California Highway 1 (CA-1) are all well-known scenic roads that run along the California coast. However, they are not the same road.

1. The Pacific Coast Highway passes through Washington, Oregon, and California.

2. The Pacific Coast Highway runs mostly along two highways: US 101 in Washington, Oregon, and parts of California and California Highway 1.

When to Drive the Pacific Coast Highway?

The best time to drive the Pacific Coast Highway depends on what you want to see and do during your trip.

If you're interested in whale watching, the best time to drive the Pacific Coast Highway is during the winter months (December to March) when gray whales migrate south to warmer waters. You can also see humpback and blue whales during this time.

If you're interested in wildflowers and greenery, the best time to drive the Pacific Coast Highway is during the spring months (April to June). During this time, you'll see hillsides covered in colorful wildflowers and lush greenery.

If you're interested in sunny weather, the best time to drive the Pacific Coast Highway is during the summer months (June to August). However, this is also the peak tourist season, so expect larger crowds and higher prices.

FREQUENTLY ASKED QUESTIONS

What is California Highway 1? What are its different names?

Pacific Coast Highway 1, also known as PCH1, is a famous coastal route in California that stretches along the Pacific Ocean. Constructed in the 1930s, this road is a masterpiece of engineering, as it closely follows the contours of the coastline, especially in central California. Pacific Coast Highway 1 is also referred to as Route 1, Highway 1, U. S. State Route 1, Shoreline Highway, and Cabrillo Highway.

How long does it take to drive the entire Pacific Coast Highway?

It depends. If you drive non-stop, it takes around 35 hours to travel from Seattle, WA to San Diego, CA via the Pacific Coast Highway. However, it's unlikely that anyone would choose to travel without any stops. Typically, driving the 1,775 miles (2857 km) of Pacific Coast Highway takes about 1-2 weeks when you include sightseeing and visiting cities along the way. To thoroughly explore this route, you might need 3-4 weeks.

Is the Pacific Coast Highway dangerous to drive?

Highway 1, particularly in Big Sur, can be dangerous due to its narrow, twisting roads and weather conditions that could cause landslides and erosion. To stay safe, drivers should take precautions such as driving slowly with fog lights on, braking gradually, and avoiding night drives in hilly areas.

FREQUENTLY ASKED QUESTIONS

Is it better to drive north or south on the Pacific Coast Highway?

When embarking on a road trip along this rugged coastline, there are two main directions to choose from: north to south or south to north. Each direction offers unique advantages and disadvantages. Ultimately, the choice comes down to personal preference and priorities.

If you choose to drive north to south, you'll be in the lane closest to the sea, providing easy access to pullouts and excellent views of the coast. However, this direction is also the most heavily trafficked and you'll be driving into the sun much of the day. This can be challenging and potentially dangerous. Nevertheless, some people may prefer this direction despite the potential drawbacks, as it offers unparalleled views of the ocean and the coastline.

On the other hand, driving south to north can be a better option for those who want to avoid heavy traffic and enjoy the views without the glare of the sun in their eyes. With the sun behind you, the coastline will be dramatically lit up, and you'll still be able to pull into viewpoint pullouts and enjoy the scenery.

The choice comes down to individual preferences and priorities. If you prioritize spectacular ocean views and don't mind heavy traffic and sun glare, driving north to south may be the way to go. But if you prefer a more leisurely pace and want to enjoy the scenery without distractions, driving south to north may be the better option.

PACIFIC COAST HIGHWAY PLAYLIST

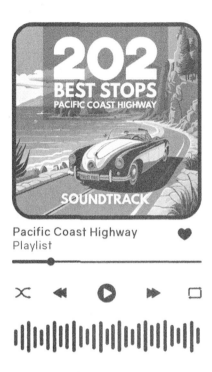

Pacific Coast Highway
Playlist

There are many hours of exploration ahead on the Pacific Coast Highway, so here is a playlist with the perfect songs to immerse you in the stunning vistas and coastal landscapes along the Pacific Coast Highway. So sit back, crank up the volume, and let the music transport you on a journey you'll never forget. Just scan the QR code using your smartphone and enjoy.

**SCAN QR CODE
AND PLAY**

DID YOU KNOW?

The Pacific Coast Highway is designated as an "All-American Road," which is the highest designation given to a scenic byway by the U.S. Department of Transportation.

The Pacific Coast Highway passes through the U.S. states of Washington, Oregon, and California.

The Pacific Coast Highway runs along two highways: US 101 in Washington, Oregon, and parts of California and California Highway 1.

The Pacific Coast Highway 1 is also referred to as Route 1, Highway 1, U. S. State Route 1, Shoreline Highway, and Cabrillo Highway.

The Pacific Coast Highway has been closed several times due to natural disasters, including landslides and wildfires.

One of the most famous stretches of the Pacific Coast Highway is the Big Sur section, which is known for its dramatic cliffs and stunning views of the Pacific Ocean.

DID YOU KNOW?

The highway has been featured in numerous films and TV shows, including *The Graduate*, *Chinatown*, and *Big Little Lies*.

The Pacific Coast Highway runs through several different climate zones, from cool and foggy in the north to warm and sunny in the south.

The Pacific Coast Highway is a popular destination for whale watching, particularly in the areas around Monterey and Santa Barbara.

The PCH is also known for its historic bridges, including the Bixby Creek Bridge in Big Sur, which is one of the most photographed bridges in the world.

The PCH has many famous surf spots, including Mavericks in Half Moon Bay and Huntington Beach in Orange County.

The PCH was originally built to provide access to coastal towns and cities and was not initially intended as a scenic highway.

PACIFIC COAST HIGHWAY MILEAGE

SEATTLE, WA TO:

Tacoma, WA .... 36 MI/58 KM	Eureka, CA .... 878 MI/1413 KM
Olympia, WA .... 53 MI/85 KM	Garberville, CA .... 953 MI/1534 KM
Sequim, WA .... 164 MI/264 KM	Leggett, CA .... 968 MI/1558 KM
Port Angeles, WA .... 180 MI/290 KM	Fort Bragg, CA .... 1011 MI/1627 KM
Forks, WA .... 237 MI/381 KM	Mendocino, CA .... 1021 MI/1643 KM
Quinault, WA .... 302 MI/486 KM	Bodega Bay, CA .... 1118 MI/1799 KM
Aberdeen, WA .... 344 MI/554 KM	San Francisco, CA .... 1186 MI/1909 KM
Long Beach, WA .... 413 MI/665 KM	Santa Cruz, CA .... 1259 MI/2026 KM
Astoria, OR .... 430 MI/682 KM	Monterey, CA .... 1303 MI/2097 KM
Cannon Beach, OR .... 454 MI/731 KM	Big Sur, CA .... 1333 MI/2145 KM
Garibaldi, OR .... 485 MI/781 KM	San Simeon, CA .... 1396 MI/2247 KM
Tillamook, OR .... 493 MI/793 KM	Morro Bay, CA .... 1426 MI/2295 KM
Lincoln City, OR .... 541 MI/871 KM	Pismo Beach, CA .... 1450 MI/2334 KM
Depoe Bay, OR .... 550 MI/885 KM	Lompoc, CA .... 1497 MI/2409 KM
Newport, OR .... 563 MI/906 KM	Santa Barbara, CA .... 1551 MI/2496 KM
Florence, OR .... 600 MI/966 KM	Ventura, CA .... 1580 MI/2546 KM
Coos Bay, OR .... 661 MI/1064 KM	Malibu, CA .... 1623 MI/2612 KM
Bandon, OR .... 685 MI/1102 KM	Santa Monica, CA .... 1635 MI/2631 KM
Port Orford, OR .... 712 MI/1146 KM	Long Beach, CA .... 1664 MI/2678 KM
Gold Beach, OR .... 739 MI/1189 KM	Huntington Beach, CA ... 1678 MI/2700 KM
Brookings, OR .... 756 MI/1217 KM	Carlsbad, CA .... 1735 MI/2792 KM
Crescent City, CA .... 794 MI/1278 KM	San Diego, CA .... 1766 MI/2842 KM

CALIFORNIA HIGHWAY 1 MILEAGE

LEGGETT, CA TO:

Westport, CA .... 27 MI/43 KM	Ragged Point, CA .... 413 MI/665 KM
Fort Bragg, CA .... 43 MI/69 KM	San Simeon, CA .... 428 MI/689 KM
Mendocino, CA .... 53 MI/85 KM	Morro Bay, CA .... 458 MI/737 KM
Point Arena, CA .... 87 MI/140 KM	San Luis Obispo, CA .... 470 MI/756 KM
Jennner, CA .... 128 MI/206 KM	Pismo Beach, CA .... 482 MI/776 KM
Bodega Bay, CA .... 150 MI/241 KM	Lompoc, CA .... 529 MI/851 KM
Marshall, CA .... 172 MI/277 KM	Santa Barbara, CA .... 583 MI/938 KM
San Francisco, CA .... 218 MI/351 KM	Ventura, CA .... 612 MI/985 KM
Pacifica, CA .... 226 MI/364 KM	Malibu, CA .... 655 MI/1054 KM
Half Moon Bay, CA .... 244 MI/393 KM	Pacific Palisades, CA .... 664 MI/1069 KM
Davenport, CA .... 282 MI/454 KM	Santa Monica, CA .... 667 MI/1074 KM
Santa Cruz, CA .... 292 MI/470 KM	Venice, CA .... 668 MI/1075 KM
Castroville, CA .... 320 MI/515 KM	Long Beach, CA .... 696 MI/1120 KM
Monterey, CA .... 335 MI/539 KM	Huntington Beach, CA .... 710 MI/1143 KM
Carmel-By-The-Sea, CA ...... 337 MI/542 KM	Newport Beach, CA .... 717 MI/1154 KM
Big Sur, CA .... 365 MI/587 KM	Laguna Beach, CA .... 727 MI/1170 KM
Plaskett, CA .... 398 MI/641 KM	Dana Point, CA .... 733 MI/1180 KM

HISTORY

THE DEVELOPMENT OF A TRANSPORTATION NETWORK CONNECTING MEXICO, THE UNITED STATES, AND CANADA BEGAN IN THE 1930S. RATHER THAN A SINGLE, UNIFIED PROJECT, THIS MULTI-STAGE ENDEAVOR INVOLVED A SERIES OF SMALLER INITIATIVES IMPLEMENTED ON A LOCAL SCALE, WITH THE AIM OF CREATING A VAST, INTERCONNECTED INFRASTRUCTURE. ONE OF THESE INITIATIVES WAS THE CONSTRUCTION OF A ROAD THAT WOULD CONNECT BEACH CITIES ALONG THE COAST. OVER TIME, THESE SHORTER SEGMENTS BECAME WHAT IS NOW KNOWN AS THE PACIFIC COAST HIGHWAY. THE PCH REMAINS ONE OF THE MOST SCENIC AND BELOVED ROADWAYS IN THE WORLD, ATTRACTING MILLIONS OF VISITORS EACH YEAR WHO COME TO EXPERIENCE THE NATURAL BEAUTY AND UNIQUE CULTURE OF THE WEST COAST. THE HIGHWAY CONTINUES TO BE A SYMBOL OF FREEDOM, ADVENTURE, AND THE AMERICAN SPIRIT.

'THE EVERGREEN STATE'

WELCOME TO
WASHINGTON
PACIFIC COAST HIGHWAY

WASHINGTON SPEED LIMITS

RURAL INTERSTATES

MPH

(*75 MPH on specific road)

URBAN INTERSTATES

SPEED LIMIT 60

MPH

OTHER LIMITED ACCESS ROADS

MPH

OTHER ROADS

MPH

SPEEDS ARE CLEARLY POSTED ALONGSIDE ROADS AND HIGHWAYS ON SIGNS OR DISPLAY PANELS. THE MAXIMUM SPEED LIMIT IN WASHINGTON IS 75 MPH (121 KM/H). NEAR RESIDENTIAL OR SCHOOL DISTRICTS, THE SPEED LIMIT CAN BE 10-25 MPH.

WELCOME TO WASHINGTON

'THE EVERGREEN STATE'
CAPITAL: OLYMPIA LARGEST CITY: SEATTLE STATEHOOD: 1889:
42ND STATE ABBREVIATION: WA LENGTH OF THE PACIFIC
COAST HIGHWAY IN THIS STATE : 427 MI / 687 KM PLACES TO
VISIT: 42 ICONIC PLACES TO VISIT: 8 OFF THE MAIN ROUTE
LOCATIONS: 4

WHERE TO PARK YOUR RV IN WASHINGTON:

This is a list with recommended RV Parks selected for a safe and comfortable stay:

RV PARKS

Blue Sky RV Park
9002 302nd Ave SE, Issaquah, WA 98027

Olympic Peninsula / Port Angeles KOA Journey
80 O Brien Rd, Port Angeles, WA 98362

Forks 101 RV Park
901 S Forks Ave, Forks, WA 98331

Big Spruce Resort RV Park & Cabin Rental
7 Riverview Dr, Hoquiam, WA 98550

Hoquiam River RV Park
425 Queen Ave, Hoquiam, WA 98550

Artic RV Park
893 US Hwy 101, Milepost 75, Cosmopolis, WA 98537

Bay Center / Willapa Bay KOA Holiday
457 Bay Center Rd, Bay Center, WA 98527

Sandcastle RV Park
1100 Pacific Ave N, Long Beach, WA 98631

RV Park At The Bridge
158 US-101, Chinook, WA 98614

WHERE TO STAY IN WASHINGTON:

MOTELS

The Grove West Seattle Inn
3512 Southwest Alaska Street, West Seattle, Seattle, WA 98126

Best Western Lakewood
6125 Motor Avenue SW, Lakewood, WA 98499

Super 8 by Wyndham Port Angeles
2104 East 1st street, Port Angeles, WA 98362

Pitchwood Inn
425 3rd Street, Raymond, WA 98577

Mermaid Inn
1910 Pacific Avenue North, Long Beach, WA 98631

Coastal Inn and Suites
620 Pacific Avenue South, Long Beach, WA 98631

HOTELS

Grand Hyatt Seattle
721 Pine St, Seattle, WA 98101, United States

Holiday Inn Express & Suites Sequim, an IHG Hotel
1441 E Washington St, Sequim, WA 98382

Lake Quinault Lodge
345 S Shore Rd, Quinault, WA 98575

Surfcrest Resort
11 Chabot Rd, Copalis Beach, WA 98535

PACIFIC COAST HWY

WASHINGTON

PLACES TO VISIT IN WASHINGTON :

1. Space Needle ☆
2. Seattle Aquarium
3. The Seattle Great Wheel
4. Pike Place Market ☆
5. The Museum of Flight
6. Pacific Bonsai Museum
7. Foss Waterway Seaport
8. Billy Frank Jr. Nisqually National Wildlife Refuge
9. Washington State Capitol
10. Hoodsport Coffee Company
11. Hama Hama Oyster Saloon
12. Mt. Walker Viewpoint
13. Port Townsend ⛺
14. Discovery Bay & Captain George Vancouver
15. Sequim Museum & Arts
16. Oak Table Cafe
17. Port Angeles City Pier ☆
18. Feiro Marine Life Center
19. Olympic National Park ☆
20. Crescent Lake Viewpoint ☆
21. Cape Flattery ⛺

22. John's Beachcombing Museum
23. Home of the Twilight
24. Forks Timber Museum
25. Hoh Rain Forest ⛺ ☆
26. Ruby Beach
27. Tree of Life ☆
28. Quinault Lake & Rain Forest
29. Seabrook ⛺
30. Hoquiam's Castle
31. Brunch 101 of Hoquiam
32. Polson Museum
33. Kurt Cobain Memorial Park
34. Clarks Restaurant
35. Northwest Carriage Museum
36. Elixir Coffee Shop
37. World's Largest Oyster
38. Long Beach Boardwalk
39. Marsh's Free Museum
40. Cape Disappointment State Park ☆
41. Fort Columbia
42. Middle Village & Station Camp

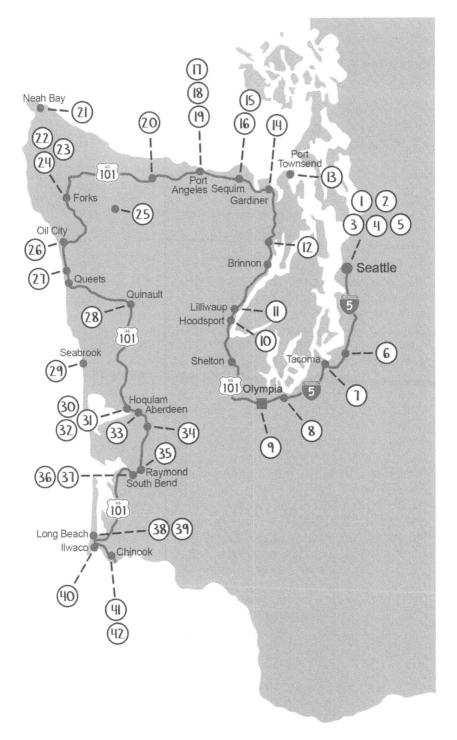

01

SPACE NEEDLE

PACIFIC COAST HWY: 0 MI/ 0 KM SEATTLE, WASHINGTON
47.62062, -122.34850

Welcome to Seattle! You are in the state of Washington. Interestingly, this state holds a unique distinction among all the states in the Union as it is the only one named after a president. Washington was nicknamed "The Evergreen State" by C.T. Conover, pioneer Seattle realtor and historian, for its abundant evergreen forests. The nickname has never been officially adopted. Soon you will travel 1775 miles (2857 km) along the Pacific Coast Highway! The beautiful city of Seattle will be your starting point for this amazing journey. It is the largest city in both the state of Washington and the Pacific Northwest region of North America, home to spectacular nature parks, sparkling waterfronts, shopping, bustling cityscapes, and coastal venues. Wake up early in the morning and start your day by visiting the Space Needle. Built in 1961, this observation tower features a deck 520 ft (160 m) above the ground, providing views of the downtown Seattle skyline, the Olympic and Cascade Mountains, Mount Rainier, Mount Baker, Elliott Bay, and various islands in Puget Sound. You can reach the top of the Space Needle by elevators, which take 41 seconds.

Space Needle
400 Broad St, Seattle, WA 98109

SCAN QR CODE TO NAVIGATE

SEATTLE AQUARIUM

PACIFIC COAST HWY: 1.4 MI/ 2.3 KM SEATTLE, WASHINGTON

47.60739, -122.34296

The next very popular attraction in this city is the Seattle Aquarium located on Pier 59. The aquarium was opened in 1977. It is home to a wide variety of marine animals, including sea otters, harbor seals, octopuses, and more. The aquarium features several exhibits that showcase the diversity and beauty of the Pacific Northwest's marine life, as well as interactive areas where visitors can touch and learn about the creatures that inhabit the local waters. One of the most popular exhibits at the Seattle Aquarium is the 120,000-gallon Window on Washington Waters, which offers a panoramic view of a simulated kelp forest ecosystem. The Seattle Aquarium is also featured as a location in the popular post-apocalyptic video game, "The Last of Us - Part II". In the game, the aquarium serves as a crucial setting for several pivotal moments in the storyline, and players get to explore both the aquarium's interior and exterior environments.

Seattle Aquarium
1483 Alaskan Way Pier 59, Seattle, WA 98101

**SCAN QR CODE
TO NAVIGATE**

TOURIST
ATTRACTION

THE SEATTLE GREAT WHEEL

PACIFIC COAST HWY: 1.4 MI/ 2.3 KM SEATTLE, WASHINGTON

47.60613, -122.34251

Situated adjacent to the Seattle Aquarium, the Seattle Great Wheel is a world-famous Ferris wheel that offers stunning views of the city's skyline, Elliott Bay, and the surrounding mountains. As an iconic Seattle landmark, it's a must-visit attraction for tourists and locals alike. This giant Ferris wheel stands 53 meters (175 feet) tall. It takes about 15 minutes for the wheel to complete a full rotation. When it opened in June 2012, it held the distinction of being the tallest Ferris wheel on the West Coast of the United States. Are you ready for a ride?

The Seattle Great Wheel
1301 Alaskan Wy, Seattle, WA 98101

**SCAN QR CODE
TO NAVIGATE**

ICONIC PLACE

TOURIST ATTRACTION

PIKE PLACE MARKET

PACIFIC COAST HWY: 1.4 MI/ 2.3 KM SEATTLE, WASHINGTON

47.60901, -122.34059

Pike Place Market is a historic public market and beloved landmark in Seattle. It was founded in 1907 and has been in continuous operation ever since. The market spans several city blocks and is home to over 500 vendors, selling everything from fresh produce and seafood to handmade crafts and artisanal foods. One of the most famous attractions at Pike Place Market is the fish market, where fishmongers famously throw fish to each other and entertain crowds of onlookers. The market also features a variety of specialty shops and restaurants, including the original first Starbucks coffee shop, which opened in 1971. Through the years, it has kept its original appearance and is guided by both design standards and historical significance. Before you hit the road, grab a cup of hot coffee! Then take Interstate 5 south.

Pike Place Market
85 Pike St, Seattle, WA 98101

**SCAN QR CODE
TO NAVIGATE**

MUSEUM

THE MUSEUM OF FLIGHT
PACIFIC COAST HWY: 8.6 MI/ 13.8 KM SEATTLE, WASHINGTON
47.51809, -122.29615

If you're interested in aviation and spaceflight, be sure to check out the Museum of Flight on the outskirts of Seattle. Located at King County International Airport, the Museum of Flight is easily accessible from Seattle. This impressive air and space museum boasts a collection of over 175 aircraft and spacecraft, including some of the most iconic planes in history. The museum was founded in 1965 and has grown to become one of the largest air and space museums in the world. Its exhibits cover the history of aviation and spaceflight, from the early days of flight to the present day. The collection includes classic and historic airplanes, such as Boeing 80A-1, Gee Bee Model Y Senior Sportster, and Douglas DC-3. The museum also includes military aircraft like a World War II-era B-17 bomber, SR-71 Blackbird spy plane, and F-14 Tomcat fighter jet. In addition to aircraft, the museum also has space artifacts, including a full-scale mockup of the Apollo Lunar Module.

The Museum of Flight
9404 E Marginal Way S, Seattle, WA 98108

**SCAN QR CODE
TO NAVIGATE**

PACIFIC BONSAI MUSEUM
PACIFIC COAST HWY: 25 MI/ 40 KM FEDERAL WAY, WASHINGTON
47.29389, -122.30200

This beautiful little museum, or I could say bonsai garden, is a hidden gem. The Pacific Bonsai Museum is dedicated to showcasing a collection of over 150 bonsai trees from around the world, including both traditional and contemporary bonsai styles. One of the trees is 200 years old! What's great is that you only need 30 minutes to see the whole bonsai exhibition. The museum is open year-round and offers free admission. Be sure to donate if you enjoy yourself (which you absolutely will).

Pacific Bonsai Museum
2515 South 336th St, Federal Way, WA 98003

**SCAN QR CODE
TO NAVIGATE**

FOSS WATERWAY SEAPORT

PACIFIC COAST HWY: 36 MI/ 58 KM TACOMA, WASHINGTON
47.25841, -122.43723

Welcome to Tacoma, situated on the shores of Commencement Bay and known for its views of Mount Rainier. Tacoma has a long history as a major port city, and its economy has historically been driven by industries such as lumber, shipping, and manufacturing. Your stop here, Foss Waterway Seaport, is a maritime museum dedicated to preserving and celebrating the rich maritime heritage of the Puget Sound region. The museum features exhibits about maritime history, culture, and technology, and offers a range of educational programs and events for all ages. The Foss Waterway Seaport is also home to a collection of historic boats definitely worth seeing. The museum is located on the waterfront, offering stunning views of the Thea Foss Waterway and the Tacoma city skyline. It is open year-round and offers affordable admission rates. Other popular attractions in Tacoma include the Museum of Glass, the Tacoma Art Museum, and the LeMay - America's Car Museum.

Foss Waterway Seaport
705 Dock St, Tacoma, WA 98402

**SCAN QR CODE
TO NAVIGATE**

08

NATURAL LANDMARK

BILLY FRANK JR. NISQUALLY NATIONAL WILDLIFE REFUGE

PACIFIC COAST HWY: 53 MI/ 85 KM OLYMPIA, WASHINGTON
47.07232, -122.71271

Before arriving at the center of Olympia, consider visiting the Billy Frank Jr. Nisqually National Wildlife Refuge. The refuge is named after Billy Frank Jr., a Nisqually tribal member who was a leading advocate for the rights of Native Americans and environmental conservation. It was established in 1974 to protect and restore the natural habitats of the Nisqually River Delta, and to provide opportunities for wildlife viewing, education, and scientific research. Visitors can explore a variety of habitats, including forests, wetlands, and mudflats, which are home to more than 300 species of birds, as well as mammals, amphibians, reptiles, and fish. A highlight for your visit is walking the mile-long Nisqually Estuary Boardwalk that extends over the estuary, making each visit different with the fluctuating tide.

Billy Frank Jr. Nisqually National Wildlife Refuge
100 Brown Farm Rd NE, Olympia, WA 98516

**SCAN QR CODE
TO NAVIGATE**

HISTORICAL LANDMARK

WASHINGTON STATE CAPITOL

PACIFIC COAST HWY: 63 MI/ 101 KM OLYMPIA, WASHINGTON
47.03614, -122.90481

Welcome to Olympia, the capital city of the state of Washington. This city has a rich history, dating back to the days of the Native American tribes who originally inhabited the area, and is a fascinating place to explore for anyone interested in the history and culture of the Pacific Northwest. The city was originally named Smithfield when it was founded in 1846, but the name was changed to Olympia in 1850 to reflect its proximity to the Olympic Mountains. Olympia is the smallest state capital in the contiguous United States by both population and land area. A visit here is a must-see destination for anyone interested in the history of the Pacific Northwest. The Capitol building features a distinctive dome made of cast iron and covered in copper that is a prominent landmark in the city. The interior of the building is decorated with ornate murals and artwork. After your visit to Olympia follow U.S. Route 101 to the next point.

Washington State Capitol Building and Campus
416 Sid Snyder Ave SW, Olympia, WA 98504

**SCAN QR CODE
TO NAVIGATE**

10

HOODSPORT COFFEE

PACIFIC COAST HWY: 98 MI/ 158 KM HOODSPORT, WASHINGTON
47.40575, -123.14080

You are now driving U.S. Route 101 along the Hood Canal and Dabob Bay, visible on your right. While you enjoy the view, take a short break at the Hoodsport Coffee Company. The cafe is known for its wide selection of coffee, sandwiches, and ice creams. They offer a variety of coffee drinks, such as lattes, cappuccinos, and Americanos. Also, the cafe building looks great with a big painted octopus on its walls. It's a popular spot for locals and visitors alike, and it's the perfect place to stop and take a break while exploring the beautiful Hood Canal and Dabob Bay area.

Hoodsport Coffee Company
24240 US-101, Hoodsport, WA 98548

**SCAN QR CODE
TO NAVIGATE**

HAMA HAMA OYSTER SALOON

PACIFIC COAST HWY: 109 MI/ 175 KM LILLIWAUP, WASHINGTON

47.54239, -123.04073

Hama Hama Oyster Saloon is a charming seafood restaurant located in Lilliwaup, WA, near the Hood Canal. The restaurant is renowned for its freshly caught and shucked oysters, which are sourced from the nearby Hama Hama Oyster Company farm. In addition to oysters, the menu also features other seafood dishes, such as smoked salmon and Pacific Northwest Dungeness crab cakes. The restaurant has a casual and relaxed atmosphere, with both indoor and outdoor seating available. Hama Hama Oyster Saloon is popular with travelers, who come for the delicious seafood, stunning views of the Hood Canal, and laid-back vibe. It's a great spot to enjoy a leisurely meal and soak up the beauty of the Pacific Northwest.

Hama Hama Oyster Saloon
35846 US-101 Suite B, Lilliwaup, WA 98555

**SCAN QR CODE
TO NAVIGATE**

MT. WALKER VIEWPOINT

PACIFIC COAST HWY: 134 MI/ 215 KM BRINNON, WASHINGTON
47.78873, -122.90573

Mt. Walker Viewpoint is perched at an elevation of 2,804 ft (855m), offering spectacular panoramic views of the surrounding area, including the Hood Canal and Olympic Mountains. The viewpoint is easily accessible by car, with a parking lot and picnic area available at the summit. There are also several hiking trails that lead to the viewpoint, ranging from easy to moderate in difficulty. The view from the top is truly breathtaking and is particularly stunning during sunset or sunrise. On clear days, visitors can see as far as Seattle and the Cascade Range. The viewpoint is a popular spot for photography, picnicking, and enjoying the beauty of the Pacific Northwest. Mt. Walker Viewpoint is a must-visit destination for anyone in the area, whether you're a seasoned hiker or simply looking for a beautiful view.

Mt. Walker Viewpoint
Mt Walker Lookout Rd, Brinnon, WA 98320

**SCAN QR CODE
TO NAVIGATE**

13

OFF THE MAIN ROUTE

HISTORICAL LANDMARK

PORT TOWNSEND

DISTANCE FROM U. S. ROUTE 101 : 13 MI / 21 KM   PORT TOWNSEND, WA
48.11695, -122.76062

This is the first location we will be visiting off the main route. Before you reach Discovery Bay, there is a junction where you'll need to turn right onto State Route 20 toward the charming coastal town of Port Townsend. In the late 1800s, there was a surge of development in Port Townsend, driven by the belief that the Pacific Northwest Railroad would be routed through the town. Although the railroad ultimately ended up in Seattle, the town's architecture remained intact, featuring stunning Victorian-style buildings that still stand today. Many of these buildings have now been designated as part of the Port Townsend National Historic Landmark District, which attracts visitors from all over the world. If you're looking to explore Port Townsend, make sure to take a stroll down Water Street. The district includes a diverse range of well-preserved homes, businesses, and public buildings, each with its own unique story to tell.

Port Townsend
Port Townsend, Washington 98368

**SCAN QR CODE
TO NAVIGATE**

14

DISCOVERY BAY &
CAPTAIN GEORGE VANCOUVER

PACIFIC COAST HWY: 152 MI/ 245 KM GARDINER, WASHINGTON
48.04607, -122.90298

There is an interesting historical marker located near U.S. Route 101 on the right side of the road. The marker provides information about Discovery Bay, Port Townsend, and Captain George Vancouver. The interpretive panel reads: "On May 2, 1792, the intrepid English explorer, Captain George Vancouver, in search of a northwest passage, sailed his sloop Discovery and the armed tender Chatham down the strait of Juan de Fuca and into this sheltered harbor. This bay Vancouver named Port Discovery for his ship, and the small island guarding the entrance he appropriately called Protection Island. While at anchor here Vancouver set out in small boats for further exploration of this vicinity and discovered nearby the harbor of Port Townsend, so named by him for the Marquis of Townshend."

Historical Marker - Discovery Bay
276669-276687 Olympic Hwy, Sequim, WA 98382

**SCAN QR CODE
TO NAVIGATE**

SEQUIM MUSEUM & ARTS
PACIFIC COAST HWY: 164 MI/ 264 KM SEQUIM, WASHINGTON
48.08398, -123.10122

Seeking a sunny spot to pause during your Pacific Coast Highway journey? Check out Sequim, located on the Olympic Peninsula in Washington. Known affectionately as "Squim," this delightful town boasts nearly 300 days of sunshine each year, earning it the nickname of "Sunny Sequim". To truly appreciate the rich history and cultural heritage of Sequim, your first port of call should be the Sequim Museum & Arts Center. The museum features exhibits on the history of the local area, including displays on the Sequim-Dungeness Valley's Native American tribes, early settlers, and local industries. Car enthusiasts won't want to miss the Sequim Museum & Arts, where a true gem of automotive history is on display: the original 1907 Reo Model B Runabout. This beautiful vehicle is just one of the many reasons to visit.

Sequim Museum & Arts
544 N Sequim Ave, Sequim, WA 98382

**SCAN QR CODE
TO NAVIGATE**

16

CAFE

OAK TABLE CAFE

PACIFIC COAST HWY: 164 MI/ 264 KM SEQUIM, WASHINGTON
48.07911, -123.10750

The Oak Table Cafe is a must-visit spot for anyone who wants to refuel after spending time at the museum. The Oak Table Cafe in Sequim is a true family affair. Mary and Billy Nagler opened the restaurant in 1981, and since then, their children Nikki, Kory, and Casey have all joined the team. Mary's brother, Billy Zuzich, is also part of the crew and serves as the general manager. Together, the family has created a warm and welcoming atmosphere where customers can enjoy a delicious meal. This is a perfect spot to grab a bite to eat or enjoy a cup of coffee. The cafe has a menu full of tasty options, including classic breakfast items, pancakes, French toast, and omelets. After enjoying a delicious meal or coffee break at the Oak Table Cafe, it's time to move on to the next leg of your journey and explore the sights and sounds of Port Angeles.

Oak Table Cafe
292 W Bell St, Sequim, WA 98382

**SCAN QR CODE
TO NAVIGATE**

PORT ANGELES CITY PIER
PACIFIC COAST HWY: 180 MI/ 290 KM PORT ANGELES, WASHINGTON
48.12097, -123.42801

Welcome to Port Angeles! Port Angeles has had several different names since its "discovery." In 1791, Lt. Francisco Eliza, a Spanish explorer, called it "El Puerto de Nuestra Señora de los Ángeles" as it provided a haven from the stormy passage through the Strait. Situated on the Olympic Peninsula, Port Angeles is known for its stunning natural beauty and outdoor recreational opportunities, including hiking, fishing, cycling, and kayaking. The city also boasts a vibrant downtown area with a variety of restaurants, shops, and galleries to explore. Commence your exploration of Port Angeles by heading to the City Pier. Take a leisurely stroll along the pier and make your way towards the end, where you'll find a viewing tower. At the top of the tower are breathtaking views of the city's harbor, as well as the Olympic Mountains and the Strait of Juan de Fuca. This is a great spot to snap some photos and get your bearings before embarking on further adventures in Port Angeles.

Port Angeles City Pier
121 E Railroad Ave, Port Angeles, WA 98362

**SCAN QR CODE
TO NAVIGATE**

18

MUSEUM

FEIRO MARINE LIFE CENTER

PACIFIC COAST HWY: 180 MI/ 290 KM PORT ANGELES, WASHINGTON

48.12022, -123.42887

This small, family-friendly aquarium situated in close proximity to Port Angeles City Pier offers a chance to learn about the marine life of the Strait of Juan de Fuca. Here, visitors can see a variety of sea creatures up close, including starfish, crabs, anemones, and fish. There are also several touch tanks where you can interact with the animals and learn about their habitats and behaviors. It is a popular destination for families with children, school groups, and anyone who is interested in marine biology or the natural beauty of the Pacific Northwest.

Feiro Marine Life Center
315 N Lincoln St, Port Angeles, WA 98362

**SCAN QR CODE
TO NAVIGATE**

ICONIC PLACE

NATURAL LANDMARK

OLYMPIC NATIONAL PARK

PACIFIC COAST HWY: 180 MI/ 290 KM PORT ANGELES, WASHINGTON

48.09929, -123.42571

Olympic National Park is an awe-inspiring national park that boasts a wide range of natural wonders, from towering peaks and lush rainforests to cascading waterfalls and scenic coastline. The park is home to a wide variety of flora and fauna, including some of the largest trees in the world, such as the Sitka spruce and Douglas fir. The Olympic National Park Visitor Center is the perfect starting point for your adventure into the park. The center offers a wide range of resources to help visitors plan their visit and make the most of their time. Inside the center, you'll find informative exhibits about the park's diverse ecosystems, wildlife, and cultural history, as well as maps and brochures to help plan your hikes, camping trips, and outdoor activities.

Olympic National Park Visitor Center
3002 Mt Angeles Rd, Port Angeles, WA 98362

**SCAN QR CODE
TO NAVIGATE**

ICONIC PLACE   NATURAL LANDMARK

LAKE CRESCENT VIEWPOINT

PACIFIC COAST HWY: 199 MI/ 320 KM MAPLE GROVE, WASHINGTON
48.07234, -123.77389

Make a quick stop at this beautiful viewpoint on Lake Crescent. This glacial lake is surrounded by stunning mountains, including Mount Storm King and Pyramid Peak. Renowned for its scenic beauty and recreational opportunities, the lake is approximately 12 miles (19 km) long and reaches a depth of up to 624 feet (190 m). It's the second deepest lake in Washington after Lake Chelan. There are many campgrounds and picnic areas around the lake, and several hiking trails provide access to the surrounding mountains and forests. I would recommend trying out the "Marymere Falls Trail," a great hiking trail with beautiful scenery. You can easily access it by parking your car at the next parking spot.

Crescent Lake Viewpoint
48.07234, -123.77389

**SCAN QR CODE
TO NAVIGATE**

21

OFF THE MAIN ROUTE

NATURAL LANDMARK

CAPE FLATTERY

DISTANCE FROM U. S. ROUTE 101 : 44 MI / 71 KM NEAH BAY. WA
48.39020, -124.71731

Nestled at the tip of the Olympic Peninsula in Washington state, Cape Flattery is a stunning destination that is worth the detour. If you're interested in visiting this breathtaking location (which I highly recommend), take a right turn at the junction in Sappho. You'll notice a gas station and a prominent sign, making it easy to spot. The driving time by car is approximately 1 hour from Sappho. Cape Flattery is the northwesternmost point of the contiguous United States. The cape is part of the Makah Reservation and is accessible via a short hiking trail that winds through the lush coastal forest. At the end of the trail, visitors are rewarded with stunning views of the Pacific Ocean and Tatoosh Island, as well as the chance to see a variety of marine wildlife such as sea otters, whales, and seabirds. Cape Flattery is also home to several historic sites, including the remnants of an old military lookout and a lighthouse that dates back to 1857. After you've taken in the stunning views at Cape Flattery, simply retrace your route back to Sappho to continue your journey.

Cape Flattery
Cape Loop Rd, Neah Bay, WA 98357

**SCAN QR CODE
TO NAVIGATE**

JOHN'S BEACHCOMBING MUSEUM

PACIFIC COAST HWY: 235 MI/ 378 KM FORKS, WASHINGTON
47.96252, -124.40135

Just before you enter the city of Forks, stop at this unusual and fascinating museum. As the name suggests, John's Beachcombing Museum is dedicated to the art of beachcombing and the treasures that can be found on the shores of the Pacific Northwest. The museum is the brainchild of John Anderson, who has been collecting beachcombing artifacts for over 50 years. His collection is one of the most extensive and diverse in the world, with over 70,000 items on display. Visitors to the museum can expect to see everything from colorful sea glass and polished stones to rare and exotic seashells, antique glass fishing floats, and even entire skeletons of marine animals. This museum is a hidden gem of the Pacific Northwest, offering a unique and awe-inspiring look at the beauty and diversity of our oceans.

John's Beachcombing Museum
143 Andersonville Ave, Forks, WA 98331

**SCAN QR CODE
TO NAVIGATE**

HOME OF THE TWILIGHT

PACIFIC COAST HWY: 237 MI/ 381 KM FORKS, WASHINGTON
47.95056, -124.38512

Welcome to Forks! Originally a logging town, Forks was established in the late 19th century. Its location on the Olympic Peninsula made it a key center for the timber industry, and the town grew rapidly in the early 20th century. Forks gained international fame in the early 2000s with the release of the "Twilight" series of novels by author Stephenie Meyer, which were set in the town. Fans of the books and subsequent movies often visit the town to see the various locations mentioned in the series. If you're interested in the Twilight franchise, you may want to explore the "Forever Twilight in Forks Collection" museum, which features memorabilia and artifacts from the saga. Additionally, you can check out the Native To Twilight gift shop for merchandise related to the series. For a unique experience, consider taking a guided tour with "Twilight Tours In Forks," which will take you to various locations in the city featured in the series.

Forever Twilight in Forks Collection
11 N Forks Ave, Forks, WA 98331

**SCAN QR CODE
TO NAVIGATE**

24

MUSEUM

FORKS TIMBER MUSEUM

PACIFIC COAST HWY: 237 MI/ 381 KM FORKS, WASHINGTON

47.93662, -124.39418

Your next stop will be The Forks Timber Museum. This small yet informative museum provides visitors with a fascinating glimpse into the history of the Pacific Northwest region's timber industry, which played a vital role in the area's economic development. The museum has a variety of exhibits, including historic photographs, tools, and logging equipment. You can also learn about the challenges and dangers that loggers faced in their work. The museum is a must-visit attraction for those interested in the history of the Pacific Northwest. The Forks Timber Museum is conveniently located near the Visitor Center, where you can obtain information on other activities and attractions to explore during your stay in Forks.

Forks Timber Museum
1421 S Forks Ave, Forks, WA 98331

**SCAN QR CODE
TO NAVIGATE**

TO VISIT
VISITED

25

 OFF THE MAIN ROUTE

 NATURAL LANDMARK

 ICONIC PLACE

HOH RAIN FOREST

DISTANCE FROM U. S. ROUTE 101: 18MI / 29KM   OLIMPIC NATIONAL PARK, WA

47.86088, -123.93483

Hoh Rain Forest is another off the main route destination located near the town of Forks. When you see the big sign for "Hoh Rainforest Olympic National Park," be sure to turn left off U.S. Route 101. You will need to drive approximately 18 miles (29 km) to reach the Visitor Center. Hoh Rain Forest is known for lush, green mosses and ferns that blanket the trees and forest floor, creating breathtaking natural scenery. The forest receives abundant rainfall throughout the year, which supports a variety of plant and animal life. Hiking trails are available for visitors to explore the forest, ranging from short, easy trails to longer, more challenging ones. The Hoh Rain Forest Visitor Center is the main starting point for exploring the Hoh Rain Forest. The Visitor Center provides helpful information and resources, such as trail maps and hiking guides. Exhibits and displays within the center also offer insight into the forest's flora and fauna. Additionally, the Visitor Center has restrooms, picnic areas, parking, and a gift shop.

Hoh Rain Forest Visitor Center
18113 Upper Hoh Rd, Forks, WA 98331

SCAN QR CODE TO NAVIGATE

NATURAL LANDMARK

RUBY BEACH

PACIFIC COAST HWY: 263 MI/ 423 KM OIL CITY, WASHINGTON
47.70739, -124.41414

Ruby Beach is the first scenic beach on our journey. The beach is named after the ruby-like crystals found in the beach sand. The area is a popular destination for photographers, hikers, and beachcombers. Ruby Beach is accessible via a short trail from the parking lot where picnic tables and restrooms are available. One of the most distinctive features of Ruby Beach is the towering sea stacks that rise up from the shoreline. These are rock formations that were once part of the headlands but have eroded over time by the sea and weather. An ideal location to capture some stunning photographs!

Ruby Beach
47.70739, -124.41414

**SCAN QR CODE
TO NAVIGATE**

ICONIC
PLACE

NATURAL
LANDMARK

TREE OF LIFE

PACIFIC COAST HWY: 270 MI/ 435 KM QUEETS, WASHINGTON

47.61318, -124.37669

To visit the famous "Tree of Life", simply park your vehicle and make your way down to the nearby beach. At the heart of this location stands the Tree of Life, a precious emblem of the enduring struggle for survival that instills a sense of courage and determination in all who behold it. But why is this tree famous? The Tree of Life, a Sitka spruce, one of Washington State's most iconic trees, is renowned for defying gravity as it seemingly grows in mid-air on a bluff overlooking the beach. With chairs and blankets in tow, you can bask in the awe-inspiring scenery and create unforgettable memories. Don't pass up the chance to visit this spot, even if it's just for a brief stop. Trust me, it's a must-see.

Tree of Life
47.61318, -124.37669

**SCAN QR CODE
TO NAVIGATE**

NATURAL LANDMARK

QUINAULT
LAKE & RAIN FOREST

PACIFIC COAST HWY: 302 MI/ 486 KM QUINAULT, WASHINGTON
47.45985, -123.86236

Quinault Lake is a large natural lake located in the Olympic National Forest. The lake is fed by a collection of small streams and surrounded by the forested hills of the Olympic Mountains. The lake is known for its clear blue water and is a popular spot for fishing, kayaking, and hiking. A lush and verdant rainforest surrounds the banks, and there are numerous hiking trails that wind their way through the forest, offering visitors the opportunity to experience the natural beauty of this unique ecosystem, as well as to see World's Largest Sitka Spruce. In addition to Quinault Lake's natural beauty and recreational opportunities, you'll also find several historic lodges and resorts, including the Lake Quinault Lodge, which was built in 1926 and is listed on the National Register of Historic Places. The lodge offers accommodations, dining, and a variety of outdoor activities, making it a popular destination for tourists visiting the Olympic Peninsula.

Quinault Rain Forest Trailhead
S Shore Rd, Quinault, WA 98575

**SCAN QR CODE
TO NAVIGATE**

SEABROOK

DISTANCE FROM U. S. ROUTE 101 : 25 MI / 40 KM SEABROOK, WA
47.19553, -124.19728

This location is off the main U. S. Route 101, but I highly recommend taking the detour as I found the next portion of Route 101 to not be very interesting. After Neilton, make a right turn and drive to the beautiful coastal town of Seabrook. Located on the rugged Washington Coast, Seabrook offers unparalleled views of the Pacific Ocean. The town of Seabrook was first founded in 2004 by Casey and Laura Roloff and has affectionately become known as Washington's Beach Town by locals and visitors alike. Inspired by Seaside, Florida, Seabrook was built with a foundation of new urbanism design where homes, shops, and restaurants are seamlessly woven into a scenic bluff overlooking the Pacific Ocean. This unique architecture features a mix of traditional and modern styles. After a visit to Seabrook the best thing is you don't need to backtrack! Simply continue on State Route 109 to Hoquiam.

Seabrook
Seabrook, Washington 98571

**SCAN QR CODE
TO NAVIGATE**

30

HISTORICAL LANDMARK

HOQUIAM CASTLE

PACIFIC COAST HWY: 340 MI/ 547 KM HOQUIAM, WASHINGTON
46.98401, -123.89077

You are in the city of Hoquiam, which has a population of around 8,500 people. The city is known for its historic downtown district, featuring many well-preserved late 19th and early 20th-century buildings. These include the Hoquiam Castle, a unique Gothic-style structure that was built in 1897 as the home of lumber baron Robert Lytle. The castle features a steeply pitched roof, pointed arches, and ornate detailing. The exterior is made of local sandstone, and the interior features intricate woodwork, stained glass windows, and other decorative elements. After Lytle's death in 1910, the castle passed through several different owners and was eventually used as a boarding house and nursing home. By the 1980s, the building had fallen into disrepair and was at risk of being demolished. However, in 1998, the city of Hoquiam purchased the castle and began a restoration project that took several years to complete. Today, the castle has been fully restored.

Hoquiam's Castle
515 Chenault Ave, Hoquiam, WA 98550

**SCAN QR CODE
TO NAVIGATE**

BRUNCH 101 OF HOQUIAM

PACIFIC COAST HWY: 340 MI/ 547 KM HOQUIAM, WASHINGTON
46.97747, -123.88476

Brunch 101 of Hoquiam is a restaurant located in the heart of downtown. The restaurant is a popular spot for locals, serving up delicious brunch dishes and a cozy, welcoming atmosphere. The brunch menu features a variety of classic breakfast dishes, such as eggs benedict, omelets, and toasts, as well as more unique options, such as huevos rancheros and Indian tacos. One of the standout features is the restaurant's commitment to using fresh, locally sourced ingredients whenever possible.

Brunch 101 of Hoquiam
716 Simpson Ave, Hoquiam, WA 98550

**SCAN QR CODE
TO NAVIGATE**

MUSEUM

POLSON MUSEUM

PACIFIC COAST HWY: 340 MI/ 547 KM HOQUIAM. WASHINGTON

46.97880, -123.88059

After enjoying a great brunch, head to the Polson Museum. The museum was founded in 1928 by local businessman Robert Polson and his wife Elizabeth, who were passionate about preserving the history of Grays Harbor County. The museum is housed in a beautiful neoclassical building originally built as a mansion in 1924. The building's architecture is just one of the many interesting features of the museum, which is home to an extensive collection of artifacts and exhibits that reveal the region's history. Visitors to the Polson Museum can explore exhibits on a variety of topics, including the logging industry, local Native American tribes, and the region's maritime history. There is also a section of the museum dedicated to the life and legacy of Robert and Elizabeth Polson, influential figures in the community.

Polson Museum
1611 Riverside Ave, Hoquiam, WA 98550

**SCAN QR CODE
TO NAVIGATE**

KURT COBAIN
MEMORIAL PARK

PACIFIC COAST HWY: 344 MI/ 554 KM ABERDEEN, WASHINGTON

46.98418, -123.80571

As you travel from Hoquiam, the next city you will reach is Aberdeen. Located in Grays Harbor County, the city is situated at the confluence of the Chehalis and Wishkah rivers, and it has a rich history that is closely tied to the region's logging and fishing industries. Aberdeen is perhaps best known as the birthplace of the musician Kurt Cobain, former lead singer of the rock band, Nirvana. Visitors to Aberdeen can visit Kurt Cobain Memorial Park which pays tribute to the musician's life and legacy.

Kurt Cobain Under the Bridge Memorial
Young St, Aberdeen, WA 98520

**SCAN QR CODE
TO NAVIGATE**

CLARKS RESTAURANT

PACIFIC COAST HWY: 351 MI/ 565 KM COSMOPOLIS, WASHINGTON
46.90580, -123.71713

Discovering small, family-run eateries along the Pacific Coast Highway is one of my favorite things. If you're a fan of homemade ice cream, don't miss out on Clark's Restaurant during your travels! Clarks started as a gas station/tavern/grocery store in 1923, and was bought by John and Beth in 1963. They served memorable Friday night dinners and homemade ice cream until retiring in 1983. Rich and Kathy bought the restaurant in 1997 and still make everything from scratch, like their burgers and hand-cut fries. They've won the "Best Burger" award 15 times. Ranie Creamer, their daughter, currently manages the restaurant. John Clark taught Kathy how to make his wonderful ice cream using his grandmother's recipe, and Kathy, in turn, passed along this knowledge to the rest of the family. Clarks still makes their shakes with the sundae on top just like John used to. The original decor has been left untouched from when the Clarks owned the restaurant to honor the memories of their longtime customers who've been coming for generations.
Come see for yourself.

Clarks Restaurant
731 U.S. 101, Cosmopolis, WA 98537

**SCAN QR CODE
TO NAVIGATE**

NORTHWEST CARRIAGE MUSEUM

PACIFIC COAST HWY: 369 MI/ 594 KM   RAYMOND, WASHINGTON
46.68344, -123.73274

In the small city of Raymond, I'd recommend visiting the Northwest Carriage Museum, dedicated to the preservation and display of historic carriages and transportation artifacts. The museum features one of the largest collections of 19th-century carriages in the United States, including a variety of horse-drawn vehicles such as coaches, sleighs, and wagons. Visitors to the museum can explore the exhibits, view historic photographs, and learn about the history of transportation in the Pacific Northwest. The Northwest Carriage Museum is a popular attraction in the area and draws visitors from across the region.

Northwest Carriage Museum
314 Alder St, Raymond, WA 98577

SCAN QR CODE
TO NAVIGATE

ELIXIR COFFEE SHOP

PACIFIC COAST HWY: 373 MI/ 600 KM SOUTH BEND, WASHINGTON

46.66607, -123.81059

It's time for coffee! Make a quick stop in South Bend, a small city situated on the banks of the Willapa River with a population of around 1,600 people. The city is known for its rich history, fishing, and logging industries, as well as scenic natural surroundings. While you're there, be sure to check out Elixir Coffee Shop, a local, family business. Elixir Coffee Shop is owned and operated by Brandon and Hannah, two talented and compassionate individuals committed to making a positive impact on people's lives. Being natives of Pacific County, they have a deep understanding of the importance of maintaining a welcoming community space. This charming cafe is nestled in one of the most scenic spots on Hwy 101, offering breathtaking views of the Willapa River and surrounding landscape. With friendly faces and a warm atmosphere, Elixir is truly a little piece of home. You can spend hours at one of their cozy tables, soaking up the scenery and savoring the delicious coffee and treats.

Elixir Coffee Shop
1015 Robert Bush Drive East, South Bend, WA 98586

**SCAN QR CODE
TO NAVIGATE**

WORLD'S LARGEST OYSTER

PACIFIC COAST HWY: 373 MI/ 600 KM SOUTH BEND, WASHINGTON
46.66634, -123.81092

Another exciting destination on our journey is located near to the Elixir Coffee Shop. South Bend is nicknamed the "Oyster Capital of the World." This small and charming city has long been a hub for oyster farming and has played a significant role in the industry's growth and success. To celebrate its reputation as the oyster capital, South Bend erected a massive, concrete statue of a halved oyster shell in Robert Bush Memorial Park. This impressive sculpture is a must-see for anyone visiting the city, and it provides a perfect opportunity to snap a memorable photo. It's worth noting that this oyster sculpture is a symbolic representation of the town's connection to the oyster industry and not intended to depict the world's largest oyster as recognized by Guinness World Records. The actual largest oyster measures nearly 14 inches (35,5 cm) in length! It can be found in Denmark and is still alive and growing! Wow!

World's Largest Oyster
1015 Robert Bush Drive East, South Bend, WA 98586

**SCAN QR CODE
TO NAVIGATE**

BEACH

LONG BEACH PENINSULA

PACIFIC COAST HWY: 413 MI/ 665 KM LONG BEACH, WASHINGTON

46.35146, -124.06237

Welcome to Long Beach! This city on the western coast of Washington state is known for having the longest continuous sandy beach in the U.S. at about 28 miles. The city is a popular tourist destination, especially during the summer months when visitors come to enjoy the beach and other outdoor activities. Some of the popular attractions in Long Beach include the World Kite Museum, the Cranberry Museum, and the Marsh's Free Museum. The city is also home to several annual events, including the International Kite Festival and the Washington State International Jet Rally.

Long Beach Boardwalk
205-203 Bolstad W, Long Beach, WA 98631

**SCAN QR CODE
TO NAVIGATE**

MUSEUM

MARSH'S FREE MUSEUM

PACIFIC COAST HWY: 413 MI/ 665 KM LONG BEACH, WASHINGTON

46.34929, -124.05530

Marsh's Free Museum is a unique and quirky museum that has been in operation since 1935. Visitors will find an eclectic collection of oddities and curiosities. One of the museum's most famous exhibits is Jake the Alligator Man, a half-man, half-alligator figure that has become a local legend. The museum also features antique arcade machines, taxidermy animals, seashells, and antique medical equipment. Marsh's Free Museum is also known for its souvenir shop, which sells a variety of items, including seashells, t-shirts, and other beach-themed merchandise. The museum and gift shop are housed in a historic building, adding to the charm and character of the attraction. Admission to Marsh's Free Museum is free, and it is open year-round. Visitors of all ages will enjoy the museum's quirky exhibits and unique atmosphere, making it a must-see attraction for anyone visiting Long Beach.

Marsh's Free Museum
409 Pacific Ave, Long Beach, WA 98631

**SCAN QR CODE
TO NAVIGATE**

ICONIC PLACE

NATURAL LANDMARK

CAPE DISAPPOINTMENT STATE PARK

PACIFIC COAST HWY: 415 MI/ 668 KM ILWACO, WASHINGTON
46.29955, -124.06538

Cape Disappointment State Park is a beautiful and historic park located on the southwestern coast of Washington State. Though Spanish explorer Bruno de Hezeta first mapped the cape in 1775, its naming is credited to English Captain John Meares, who approached the cape in 1788, but could not locate the river's entrance. The park offers stunning views of the Pacific Ocean, the Columbia River, and the rugged cliffs and forested hills. Visitors can explore its many hiking trails, campgrounds, and beaches, as well as two lighthouses: the North Head Lighthouse, which has been in operation since 1898, and historic Cape Disappointment Lighthouse, which has been in operation since 1856 and remains an important navigation aid for ships encountering the treacherous waters of the Columbia River Bar. Also worth seeing are Fort Canby and the Lewis and Clark Interpretive Center which showcases the famous explorers' journey to the area.

Cape Disappointment State Park
244 Robert Gray Dr, Ilwaco, WA 98624

**SCAN QR CODE
TO NAVIGATE**

FORT COLUMBIA

PACIFIC COAST HWY: 424 MI/ 682 KM CHINOOK, WASHINGTON

46.25332, -123.91878

Fort Columbia is a historic military fort located near the town of Chinook. Military and maritime history buffs, take note! Fort Columbia State Park is considered one of the most intact historic coastal defense sites in the U.S. Its construction began in 1896 and was renovated during World War II before it was decommissioned in 1947. Today, visitors can experience what life was like during this period in the early 20th century. Among the notable sights are the officer's homes, artillery batteries, and six World War II-era guns. Two 6-inch rapid-fire guns are among the highlights of the park, having been transferred from a U.S. Navy facility in Newfoundland in 1994. The park's interpretive center features a collection of artifacts, photos, and stories about the military community on the Columbia River, as well as the area's exploration and fur trade. Visitors can learn about the history of the region and how it contributed to the development of the Pacific Northwest.

Fort Columbia
Chinook Point, Chinook, WA 98614

**SCAN QR CODE
TO NAVIGATE**

HISTORICAL
LANDMARK

MIDDLE VILLAGE & STATION CAMP

PACIFIC COAST HWY: 425 MI/ 684 KM CHINOOK, WASHINGTON

46.24677, -123.91009

Right along U. S. Route 101 on the north side of the Columbia River and east of Chinook, you'll find Middle Village. This is the site of a significant Chinook village that served as an important trade hub for thousands of years. Prior to Lewis and Clark's arrival, almost 90 trade ships crossed the Columbia River Bar to trade with Native Americans for beaver and sea otter pelts. The Lewis and Clark Corps of Discovery used Middle Village as a departure point for their overland trek to the Pacific Ocean and also stayed at "Station Camp," where they produced a detailed map of the mouth of the Columbia River. In 2012, the Middle Village - Station Camp historical site was dedicated and now focuses on the history of the Chinook people and their interactions with early explorers.

Middle Village - Station Camp
354 US-101, Chinook, WA 98614

**SCAN QR CODE
TO NAVIGATE**

'THE BEAVER STATE'

OREGON SPEED LIMITS

RURAL INTERSTATES

(*70 MPH on specific road)

URBAN INTERSTATES

OTHER LIMITED
ACCESS ROADS

OTHER ROADS

SPEEDS ARE CLEARLY POSTED ALONGSIDE ROADS AND HIGHWAYS ON SIGNS OR DISPLAY PANELS. THE MAXIMUM SPEED LIMIT IN OREGON IS 65 MPH (105 KM/H). NEAR RESIDENTIAL OR SCHOOL DISTRICTS, THE SPEED LIMIT CAN BE 10-25 MPH.

OREGON

'THE BEAVER STATE'
CAPITAL: **SALEM** LARGEST CITY: **PORTLAND** STATEHOOD: 1859:
33RD STATE ABBREVIATION: **OR** LENGTH OF THE PACIFIC
COAST HIGHWAY IN THIS STATE : **344 MI / 554 KM** PLACES TO
VISIT: **43** ICONIC PLACES TO VISIT: **8** OFF THE MAIN ROUTE
LOCATIONS: **3**

WHERE TO PARK YOUR RV IN OREGON:

This is a list with recommended RV Parks selected for a safe and comfortable stay:

RV PARKS

Lewis & Clark Golf & RV Park
92294 Youngs River Rd, Astoria, OR 97103

Circle Creek RV Resort
85658 US-101, Seaside, OR 97138

RV Resort at Cannon Beach
340 Elk Creek Rd, Cannon Beach, OR 97110

Cape Kiwanda RV Park
33305 Cape Kiwanda Dr, Pacific City, OR 97135

Devils Lake RV Park
4041 NE West Devils Lake Rd, Lincoln City, OR 97367

Sea & Sand RV Park
4985 N US-101, Depoe Bay, OR 97341

Seal Rocks RV Cove
1276 NW Cross St, Seal Rock, OR 97376

Cypress Hills RV Campground
48203 US-101, Langlois, OR 97450

Honey Bear by the Sea RV Resort and Campground
34161 Ophir Rd, Gold Beach, OR 97444

AtRivers Edge RV Resort
98203 S Bank Chetco River Rd, Brookings, OR 97415

WHERE TO STAY IN OREGON:

MOTELS

Ebb Tide Oceanfront Inn
300 North Prom, Seaside, OR 97138

Sunset Surf Motel
248 Ocean Road, Manzanita, OR 97130

Harborview Inn & RV Park
302 South 7th Street, Garibaldi, OR 97118

The Waldport Inn
190 U.S. 101 P.O.Box 871, Waldport, OR 97394

Park Motel and Cabins
85034 Highway 101 South, Florence, OR 97439

Westward Inn
1026 Chetco Avenue, Brookings, OR 97415

HOTELS

Headlands Coastal Lodge & Spa
33000 Cape Kiwanda Drive, Pacific City, OR 97135

The Coho Oceanfront Lodge
1635 NorthWest Harbor, Lincoln City, OR 97367

Surfland Hotel
2133 NW Inlet Ave, Lincoln City, 97367

Starfish Point
140 NW 48th Street, Newport, OR 97365

Beachfront Inn
16008 Boat Basin Road, Brookings, OR 97415-8307

PACIFIC COAST HWY

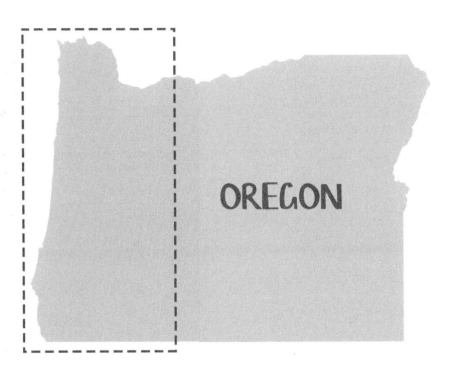

OREGON

PLACES TO VISIT IN OREGON :

(43) Astoria-Megler Bridge

(44) The Astoria Column ☆

(45) Columbia River Maritime Museum

(46) Bridgewater Bistro

(47) Lewis and Clark National Historical Park

(48) Fort Stevens State Park ⛺

(49) Pacific Way Cafe

(50) Painted Rock Beach

(51) Ecola State Park ⛺

(52) Haystack Rock ☆

(53) Neahkahnie Viewpoint

(54) Wanda's Cafe + Bakery

(55) Oregon Coast Scenic Railroad

(56) Tillamook Creamery

(57) Cape Kiwanda State Natural Area ⛺

(58) Neskowin Ghost Forest

(59) North Lincoln County Historical Museum

(60) Tidal Raves

(61) Lookout Observatory and Gift Shop

(62) Devils Punchbowl State Natural Area

(63) Yaquina Head Lighthouse ☆

(64) Local Ocean Seafoods

(65) Pacific Maritime Heritage Center

(66) Oregon Coast Aquarium

(67) Seal Rock State Recreation Site

(68) Thor's Well ☆

(69) Hobbit Trail

(70) Heceta Head Lighthouse ☆

(71) Sea Lion Caves ☆

(72) Oregon Dunes

(73) Coos History Museum & Maritime Collection

(74) Bandon Coffee Cafe

(75) Bandon Historical Society Museum

(76) Face Rock State Scenic Viewpoint

(77) Something Awesome

(78) Hawthorne Gallery

(79) Port Orford Overlook View Point

(80) Jerry's Rogue Jets

(81) Port Hole Cafe

(82) Kissing Rock

(83) Arch Rock State Park ☆

(84) Secret Beach ☆

(85) Harris Beach State Park

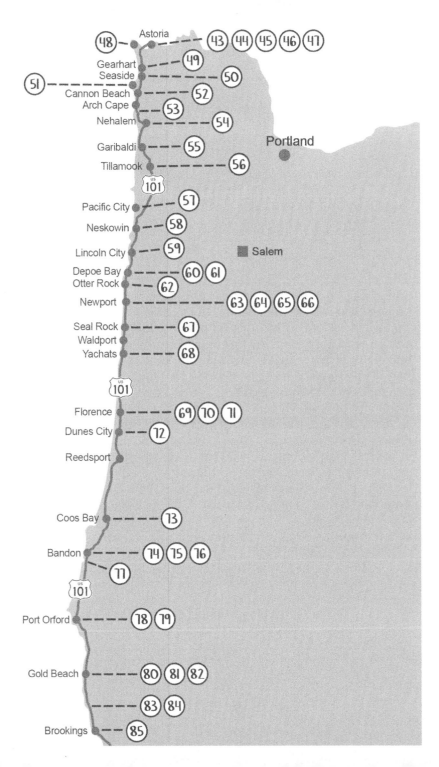

ASTORIA-MEGLER BRIDGE

PACIFIC COAST HWY: 430 MI/ 692 KM ASTORIA, OREGON
46.21576, -123.86223

Welcome to the state of Oregon commonly known as "The Beaver State." The nickname dates back to the early days of the state when beaver fur was a valuable commodity and the animal was abundant in Oregon's streams and wetlands. The beaver is also the state animal and is featured on the state flag. The Oregon Coast is famous for its rugged cliffs, sandy beaches, and stunning vistas, and it stretches for 363 miles along the Pacific Ocean. Your first city to visit in Oregon is Astoria. You'll enter by crossing the beautiful Astoria-Megler Bridge. The bridge was opened to traffic on July 28, 1966 and is a vital transportation link for the region. This impressive engineering feat spans a total length of 4.1 miles (6.6 km), making it the longest continuous truss bridge in North America. It has a main span of 1,232 feet (375 m) and a maximum vertical clearance of 200 feet (61 m) to accommodate large ships passing underneath. The bridge provides a stunning view of the Columbia River and is an important part of the U.S. Route 101 highway.

Astoria-Megler Bridge
US-101, Astoria, OR 97103

**SCAN QR CODE
TO NAVIGATE**

TO VISIT
VISITED

44

ICONIC PLACE

HISTORICAL LANDMARK

THE ASTORIA COLUMN

PACIFIC COAST HWY: 430 MI/ 692 KM ASTORIA, OREGON

46.18132, -123.81752

You've arrived in Astoria – welcome! This is the oldest city in the state of Oregon, founded in 1811 by fur traders from the Pacific Fur Company. The city is named after John Jacob Astor, a wealthy fur trader who financed the establishment of the Pacific Fur Company. Start your visit to the city with a trip to the Astoria Column a 125-foot-tall (38 meters) tower located on Coxcomb Hill. It was built in 1926 to commemorate the discovery of the Columbia River by Captain Robert Gray in 1792 and to honor the early pioneers of the region. The column is made of concrete and decorated with murals depicting important events in the history of Oregon. You can climb a spiral staircase to the top of the column, where you'll enjoy panoramic views of the city, the Columbia River, and the surrounding mountains and forests. The Astoria Column is one of the most popular tourist attractions in the city and is open to the public year-round.

The Astoria Column
1 Coxcomb Dr, Astoria, OR 97103

**SCAN QR CODE
TO NAVIGATE**

TO VISIT
VISITED

 MUSEUM

COLUMBIA RIVER MARITIME MUSEUM

PACIFIC COAST HWY: 430 MI/ 692 KM ASTORIA, OREGON
46.18988, -123.82360

The Columbia River Maritime Museum is dedicated to the maritime history of the Columbia River and the Pacific Northwest. The museum features a collection of over 30,000 objects, including historic boats, ship models, maritime artifacts, photographs, and documents. You can explore a variety of exhibits that showcase the region's rich maritime heritage. One of the museum's most popular exhibits is the Lightship Columbia, which is moored next to the museum and is open for tours. The Lightship Columbia served as a floating lighthouse on the Columbia River Bar from 1951 to 1979, and is now a National Historic Landmark.

Columbia River Maritime Museum
1792 Marine Dr, Astoria, OR 97103

**SCAN QR CODE
TO NAVIGATE**

46

RESTAURANT

BRIDGEWATER BISTRO

PACIFIC COAST HWY: 430 MI/ 692 KM ASTORIA, OREGON

46.18958, -123.85161

After exploring all the attractions in Astoria, it's time to grab a bite to eat. Before continuing on your journey, make sure to visit Bridgewater Bistro. Located in a restored 1896 building, the restaurant overlooks the Columbia River from a pier. They feature Pacific Northwest cuisine with an emphasis on fresh, locally sourced ingredients. Bridgewater Bistro's menu includes a variety of seafood dishes, including Dungeness crab, shrimps, and grilled salmon. The restaurant also serves vegetarian options like salads and pasta. I highly recommend visiting this place during sunset for the beautiful views and great photo opportunities!

Bridgewater Bistro
20 Basin St Ste. A, Astoria, OR 97103

**SCAN QR CODE
TO NAVIGATE**

LEWIS AND CLARK
NATIONAL HISTORICAL PARK

PACIFIC COAST HWY: 435 MI/ 700 KM ASTORIA, OREGON

46.13450, -123.88031

Lewis and Clark National Historical Park preserves and interprets the historic expedition of Meriwether Lewis and William Clark, who led the first American overland expedition to the Pacific Coast in 1804-1806. The park is divided into two main areas: the Fort Clatsop unit in Oregon, which includes a replica of the fort where the expedition wintered, and the Cape Disappointment unit in Washington, which includes several sites visited by the expedition and a museum. The Fort Clatsop unit is located near the mouth of the Columbia River, where the expedition established their winter encampment in 1805-1806. Visitors can tour the fort replica, explore the trails and exhibits, and learn about the challenges and achievements of the expedition through interactive displays and ranger-led programs.

Lewis and Clark National Historical Park
92343 Fort Clatsop Rd, Astoria, OR 97103

**SCAN QR CODE
TO NAVIGATE**

OFF THE MAIN ROUTE

NATURAL LANDMARK

FORT STEVENS STATE PARK

DISTANCE FROM U. S. ROUTE 101 : 6 MI / 10 KM HAMMOND, OR

46.19937, -123.97906

Fort Stevens State Park is a popular recreational area located on the northern coast of Oregon in the United States. The park is situated on a historic military reservation that was once used to defend the Columbia River and nearby cities during World War II. Today, visitors can explore the park's military history and hike through its scenic forests and dunes. One of the park's main attractions is the historic shipwreck of the Peter Iredale, which ran aground on the beach in 1906 and can still be seen today. To reach Fort Stevens State Park, you'll need to take a slight detour, but the ride should only take about 8 minutes.

Fort Stevens State Park
1675 Peter Iredale Rd, Hammond, OR 97121

**SCAN QR CODE
TO NAVIGATE**

PACIFIC WAY CAFE

PACIFIC COAST HWY: 444 MI/ 715 KM GEARHART, OREGON

46.02396, -123.92023

Traveling south along the coast, you'll pass through several charming coastal villages. The first one you'll come across is Gearhart, an ideal spot to take a break and enjoy a cup of coffee. The Pacific Way Cafe is cozy and welcoming, known for its delicious coffee and baked goods. The cafe features a warm and inviting atmosphere with friendly staff. After getting your coffee at the Pacific Way Cafe, I highly recommend taking a short stroll over to the Lesley Miller Dunes Meadow Park, which is just a few steps away. This lovely park offers breathtaking views of the nearby seaside and is a great place to relax and soak in the natural beauty of the Oregon coast while sipping your coffee.

Pacific Way Cafe & Marketplace
601-609 Pacific Way, Gearhart, OR 97138

**SCAN QR CODE
TO NAVIGATE**

PAINTED ROCK BEACH

PACIFIC COAST HWY: 447 MI/ 719 KM SEASIDE, OREGON
45.97852, -123.93537

Nestled away from the sandy shores at the far end of the town's southern limits lies a delightful collection of brightly painted stones, now a beloved attraction in Seaside. While some of the area's residents may have lost touch with its origins, both tourists and locals continue to appreciate the tradition and charm of Painted Rock Beach. It features a gravel footpath, fine sand, beach grass, and a humble wooden bench on a stone brick patio with serene landscapes and seascapes. Visitors can relax, take photos, and admire the decorated rocks. It's a perfect spot for those who want to create their own artistic rocks or enjoy a peaceful getaway.

Painted Rock Beach
2477-2401 Ocean Vista Dr, Seaside, OR 97138

**SCAN QR CODE
TO NAVIGATE**

51

OFF THE MAIN ROUTE

NATURAL LANDMARK

ECOLA STATE PARK

DISTANCE FROM U. S. ROUTE 101 : 2 MI / 3 KM CANNON BEACH, OR

45.91946, -123.97375

Ecola State Park is a scenic park located on the northern Oregon coast in the United States. It is known for its stunning views of the Pacific Ocean and the surrounding rugged coastline. The park covers an area of over 1,000 acres and offers a variety of outdoor recreational activities for visitors to enjoy. One of the main attractions of Ecola State Park is the hiking trails that wind through the park's lush forests and along the rugged coastline with views of Haystack Rock, a Tillamook Lighthouse, and isolated beaches. The park has several trails of varying difficulty, ranging from easy walks to strenuous hikes. Ecola State Park is open year-round and is located just ten minutes north of the town of Cannon Beach. The park has a small entrance fee, and camping is available at nearby campgrounds.

Ecola State Park
Ecola Park Rd, Cannon Beach, OR 97110

**SCAN QR CODE
TO NAVIGATE**

HAYSTACK ROCK

PACIFIC COAST HWY: 454 MI/ 731 KM CANNON BEACH, OREGON
45.88452, -123.96819

Cannon Beach is a beautiful coastal city famous for its stunning coastline, towering sea stacks, and expansive sandy beaches. One of the most iconic landmarks in Cannon Beach is Haystack Rock, a 235-foot (72 meters) sea stack located near the shore. This awe-inspiring natural wonder rises majestically from the Pacific Ocean, offering a truly mesmerizing sight to all who behold it. The beach surrounding the rock is equally stunning, with an expansive shoreline and pristine sand perfect for taking long, leisurely strolls.

Haystack Rock
45.88450, -123.96823

**SCAN QR CODE
TO NAVIGATE**

53

NEAHKAHNIE VIEWPOINT

PACIFIC COAST HWY: 465 MI/ 748 KM ARCH CAPE, OREGON
45.74455, -123.96080

Neahkahnie Viewpoint is a scenic lookout located next to the Oswald West State Park. It offers panoramic views of the Pacific Ocean and the surrounding coastline, making it a popular destination for travelers along U.S. Route 101. At Neahkahnie Viewpoint, visitors can take in stunning vistas of the ocean, beach, and rock formations unique to this part of the coast. The viewpoint is perched high on a cliff, providing a bird's eye view of the surrounding landscape. On a clear day, you can even see as far as Cape Lookout. Nearby Oswald West State Park is also worth seeing. It features several hiking trails, including the Cape Falcon Trail (I highly suggest you give this a try), which leads to a scenic viewpoint overlooking the ocean. Visitors can also explore the park's lush forests and creeks, home to a variety of wildlife. Now, let your binoculars bring the view into sharper focus and marvel at the sights before you.

Neahkahnie Viewpoint
Oswald West State Park, Arch Cape, OR 97102

**SCAN QR CODE
TO NAVIGATE**

WANDA'S CAFE + BAKERY

PACIFIC COAST HWY: 470 MI/ 756 KM NEHALEM, OREGON

45.71790, -123.89653

Wanda's Cafe + Bakery is a family-owned and operated establishment that has been serving the Oregon Coast community since 1999. With their commitment to quality ingredients and friendly service, Wanda's has become a beloved spot for locals and Pacific Coast Highway travelers alike. They offer a variety of breakfast dishes as well as a selection of baked goods and good coffee. Popular menu items at Wanda's Cafe + Bakery include omelets, sandwiches and granola. The cafe is also known for their delicious baked goods, which include a variety of pies, cakes, and cookies. Not only a great spot for a quick stop, but also a destination worth visiting in its own right. With its cozy and welcoming atmosphere, friendly service, and delicious menu of breakfast dishes and baked goods, Wanda's is the perfect place to sit down, relax, and enjoy a meal with friends or family.

Wanda's Cafe + Bakery
12880 H St, Nehalem, OR 97131

**SCAN QR CODE
TO NAVIGATE**

55

TOURIST
ATTRACTION

OREGON COAST
SCENIC RAILROAD

PACIFIC COAST HWY: 485 MI/ 781 KM GARIBALDI, OREGON

45.55867, -123.91145

Welcome to the village of Garibaldi. It was named after Giuseppe Garibaldi, an Italian military and political figure who played a key role in the unification of Italy in the 19th century. The town of Garibaldi was named by Captain Robert Gray, an American explorer who discovered the area in the late 18th century. Gray was a fan of Garibaldi and named the town after him as a tribute to his revolutionary spirit and leadership. Today, Garibaldi is a popular destination for visitors to the Oregon Coast, with its scenic beauty, historic sites, and charming small-town atmosphere. You can explore the Garibaldi Museum, which houses exhibits on the area's maritime history, or take a ride on the historic steam-powered train, the Oregon Coast Scenic Railroad. The train takes about a half hour to go from Garibaldi to Rockaway beach with about 20 minutes to walk around before returning.

Oregon Coast Scenic Railroad
402 American Ave, Garibaldi, OR 97118

**SCAN QR CODE
TO NAVIGATE**

TOURIST
ATTRACTION

TILLAMOOK CREAMERY

PACIFIC COAST HWY: 493 MI/ 793 KM TILLAMOOK, OREGON
45.48398, -123.84426

Tillamook is known for its famous cheese, produced by the Tillamook County Creamery Association. Time to take a break from driving and have some fun at this next destination on your road trip! Tillamook Creamery was founded in 1909 as a way for local dairy farmers to combine their resources and improve the quality of their products. Today, it is known for its high-quality dairy products, including cheese, ice cream, butter, and yogurt. The creamery offers tours where you can see how its products are made, sample cheese and ice cream, and learn about the history of the cooperative. Tillamook city is also home to several other attractions, including the Tillamook Air Museum, which features vintage aircraft and exhibits on aviation history, and the Tillamook County Pioneer Museum, which showcases the area's history and culture through exhibits and artifacts.

Tillamook Creamery
4165 N Hwy 101, Tillamook, OR 97141

**SCAN QR CODE
TO NAVIGATE**

CAPE KIWANDA
STATE NATURAL AREA

DISTANCE FROM U. S. ROUTE 101: 5 MI / 8 KM PACIFIC CITY, OR
45.21905, -123.97530

Attention photographers and Instagram enthusiasts: You won't want to miss this next destination - it's a picture-perfect paradise! Cape Kiwanda State Natural Area is a popular coastal recreation area located on the Oregon Coast in Pacific City. It is known for its beautiful sandy beaches, towering sand dunes, and stunning ocean views. The area is part of the larger Three Capes Scenic Route, which runs along the coast and includes Cape Meares and Cape Lookout State Parks. The area is home to several hiking trails, including the challenging Cape Kiwanda Trail, which provides panoramic views of the ocean and surrounding landscape. Cape Kiwanda is also known for its unique geological features, like the famous "Chief Kiwanda Rock," a large formation just offshore.

Cape Kiwanda State Natural Area
Cape Kiwanda State Natural Area, Pacific City, OR 97135

**SCAN QR CODE
TO NAVIGATE**

NESKOWIN GHOST FOREST

PACIFIC COAST HWY: 526 MI/ 847 KM NESKOWIN, OREGON

45.09560, -123.98869

The Neskowin Ghost Forest is a unique and fascinating natural wonder located in the small coastal town of Neskowin. The "ghost forest" is a group of ancient tree stumps preserved by sand and mud for centuries and estimated to be more than 2,000 years old. The stumps were likely part of a coastal forest that was buried by a massive earthquake and tsunami off the Oregon coast more than 2,000 years ago. Over time, the ocean eroded the sand and mud that covered the stumps, exposing them to the elements and creating the eerie and haunting landscape seen today. The Neskowin Ghost Forest is accessible during low tide, and I recommend you visit during the early morning or late evening hours when the sun is low in the sky for the best lighting and photo opportunities.

Neskowin Ghost Forest
Seasand Cir, Neskowin, OR 97149

**SCAN QR CODE
TO NAVIGATE**

MUSEUM

NORTH LINCOLN COUNTY HISTORICAL MUSEUM

PACIFIC COAST HWY: 541 MI/ 871 KM LINCOLN CITY, OREGON
44.92901, -124.01617

You've arrived in Lincoln City! Situated on the Pacific Ocean, it's known for beautiful beaches, stunning views, and outdoor recreation opportunities. Lincoln City was incorporated in 1965 and has a population of around 9,000 people. One of the most popular attractions in the city is the North Lincoln County Historical Museum. The museum is dedicated to preserving and showcasing the history and culture of North Lincoln County, which includes the towns of Lincoln City, Depoe Bay, Gleneden Beach, Otis, Neskowin, and Neotsu. The museum's collection includes artifacts, photographs, documents, and other memorabilia that tell the story of the area's early settlers, Native American tribes, logging industry, fishing industry, tourism, and other important aspects of the region's past. The museum is open year-round, and admission is free, though donations are appreciated.

North Lincoln County Historical Museum
4907 Oregon Coast Hwy, Lincoln City, OR 97367

**SCAN QR CODE
TO NAVIGATE**

RESTAURANT

TIDAL RAVES

PACIFIC COAST HWY: 550 MI/ 885 KM DEPOE BAY, OREGON

44.81534, -124.06279

Tidal Raves is a popular restaurant located in Depoe Bay, Oregon. Known for its stunning views of the Pacific Ocean and fresh seafood, it's a must-visit destination for all hungry Pacific Coast Highway travelers. The restaurant's menu features a variety of seafood dishes, including Dungeness crab, salmon, halibut, and oysters. Non-seafood options are also available, such as sandwiches and salads. The restaurant is perched on a cliff overlooking the ocean, providing diners with breathtaking views of the waves crashing against the rocks below. The cozy interior is perfect for a romantic evening or special occasion.

Tidal Raves Seafood Grill
279 US-101, Depoe Bay, OR 97341

**SCAN QR CODE
TO NAVIGATE**

TOURIST
ATTRACTION

LOOKOUT OBSERVATORY AND GIFT SHOP

PACIFIC COAST HWY: 554 MI/ 892 KM   DEPOE BAY, OREGON

44.76041, -124.06700

If you're looking for a picturesque spot to take stunning photos and soak in the beauty of Oregon's coast, be sure to add The Lookout Observatory and Gift Shop to your must-visit list! Nestled on a cliff in a charming wooden building, this place is truly breathtaking! You'll be treated to a sweeping panoramic view of the entire coast, from the lighthouse on one end to the northern coast on the other. Large windows allow for stunning views while staying cozy inside. And if you're in the mood for souvenir shopping, you'll find a delightful gift shop inside as well. Keep in mind this spot is only open during season, but don't let that keep you from stopping by to capture some amazing photos of the stunning scenery.

Lookout Observatory and Gift Shop
4905 Otter Crest Loop, Depoe Bay, OR 97341

**SCAN QR CODE
TO NAVIGATE**

DEVILS PUNCHBOWL STATE NATURAL AREA

PACIFIC COAST HWY: 555 MI/ 893 KM OTTER ROCK, OREGON
44.74713, -124.06518

Devils Punchbowl State Natural Area is a beautiful and unique park located in Otter Rock, Oregon. Named after the main attraction of the park, The Devils Punchbowl is a large bowl-shaped depression in the rock that is fills with water during high tide. You can hike down to the beach and explore the area around the Punchbowl during low tide, but exercise caution during high tide as the area can be dangerous. The park is open year-round and admission is free, although there is a fee for parking. The Devils Punchbowl is a popular destination for photographers and nature enthusiasts, who come to marvel at the power and beauty of the Pacific Ocean. It's time to channel your inner photographer and capture some beautiful moments. Take out your smartphone or camera and start shooting!

Devils Punchbowl Arch
1st St, Otter Rock, OR 97369

**SCAN QR CODE
TO NAVIGATE**

YAQUINA HEAD LIGHTHOUSE

PACIFIC COAST HWY: 561 MI/ 903 KM NEWPORT, OREGON

44.67679, -124.07956

While traveling down the Pacific Coast Highway, you'll have the opportunity to see numerous lighthouses, but this one is definitely a standout and shouldn't be overlooked. Yaquina Head Lighthouse stands 93 feet (28 m) tall and has been in operation since 1873. The lighthouse is situated on a rocky headland overlooking the Pacific Ocean and offers stunning views of the coastline. You can take a guided tour and learn about the lighthouse's fascinating history and the role it played in maritime navigation. One of the highlights of visiting Yaquina Head Lighthouse is the opportunity to spot wildlife such as whales, sea lions, and seabirds. It's a popular spot to observe the annual gray whale migration from December to June.

Yaquina Head Lighthouse
750 NW Lighthouse Dr, Newport, OR 97365

**SCAN QR CODE
TO NAVIGATE**

TO VISIT
VISITED

LOCAL OCEAN SEAFOODS

PACIFIC COAST HWY: 563 MI/ 906 KM NEWPORT, OREGON

44.63205, -124.04906

Welcome to Newport, a charming coastal city situated on the beautiful central Oregon coast. One of the highlights of Newport is its picturesque harbor, home to a thriving fishing industry and a variety of seafood restaurants. You can watch the fishing boats come in and sample fresh seafood, including Dungeness crab, Pacific oysters, and wild-caught salmon. Are you a seafood lover? If so, then you must visit Local Ocean Seafoods for some of the best seafood around! This place began as a fish market with a small restaurant, but expanded due to popular demand. The owners are passionate about sustainable seafood and work closely with local fishermen and farmers to ensure the highest quality ingredients. The restaurant takes pride in every dish they serve and has a deep connection to the local fishing community. Customers can taste the care and attention in every bite, and the restaurant has become a popular destination for fresh, local seafood.

Local Ocean Seafoods
213 SE Bay Blvd., Newport, OR 97365

**SCAN QR CODE
TO NAVIGATE**

☐ TO VISIT
☐ VISITED

65

MUSEUM

PACIFIC MARITIME HERITAGE CENTER

PACIFIC COAST HWY: 563 MI/ 906 KM NEWPORT, OREGON
44.63260, -124.04849

If you're looking for a captivating experience after indulging in Newport's scrumptious cuisine, the Pacific Maritime Heritage Center should be your next port of call. With its engaging exhibits and displays, the center offers an unparalleled opportunity to delve into the region's captivating maritime heritage and discover the profound impact of the sea on the local way of life. Located in an impressive building on Newport's historic Bayfront, the building and site were purchased by the Lincoln County Historical Society in 2004.

Pacific Maritime Heritage Center
333 SE Bay Blvd., Newport, OR 97365

**SCAN QR CODE
TO NAVIGATE**

OREGON COAST AQUARIUM

PACIFIC COAST HWY: 564 MI/ 908 KM NEWPORT, OREGON
44.61770, -124.04729

Experience the perfect blend of excitement and education by visiting the Oregon Coast Aquarium, a must-see attraction in Newport. Established in 1992, the aquarium features a diverse collection of over 15,000 animals representing over 250 species, including otters, seals, sea lions, sea birds, and a variety of fish and invertebrates. You can explore a range of exhibits, including the Passages of the Deep, where you can walk through a glass tunnel surrounded by sharks, rays, and other marine creatures. The aquarium also has an interactive Touch Pool exhibit, where you can get up close and personal with sea stars, sea anemones, and other invertebrates. The Oregon Coast Aquarium is committed to promoting ocean conservation and educating visitors about the importance of protecting our marine ecosystems.

Oregon Coast Aquarium
2820 SE Ferry Slip Rd, Newport, OR 97365

**SCAN QR CODE
TO NAVIGATE**

NATURAL
LANDMARK

SEAL ROCK STATE RECREATION SITE

PACIFIC COAST HWY: 574 MI/ 924 KM SEAL ROCK, OREGON

44.49734, -124.08267

Seal Rock State Recreation Site is a beautiful coastal park located along the Oregon Coast Highway. The park is named after the nearby Seal Rock formation, a series of large rocks jutting out of the ocean. The formation is made up of basalt rock estimated to be between 10 and 20 million years old. Take a stroll along the beach and watch the waves crash against the rocks. Whether you're a professional photographer or just enjoy taking snapshots on your smartphone, you'll be able to capture some truly beautiful images at this scenic location. Just be sure to exercise caution and stay a safe distance from the waves, as the currents can be quite strong and dangerous.

Seal Rock State Recreation Site
10032 NW Pacific Coast Hwy, Seal Rock, OR 97376

**SCAN QR CODE
TO NAVIGATE**

ICONIC PLACE

NATURAL LANDMARK

THOR'S WELL

PACIFIC COAST HWY: 590 MI/ 950 KM YACHATS, OREGON
44.27836, -124.11347

Thor's Well is a natural wonder that's part of the Cape Perpetua National Forest. This large, circular sinkhole appears to be a bottomless pit, constantly draining and refilling with seawater. The well is approximately 20 feet deep (6 meters) and during high tide, waves crash into the hole, creating dramatic spouts of water that shoot up to 20 feet (6 meters) in the air. The water drains back down into the hole, and then the cycle repeats. While Thor's Well is a beautiful and unique sight to see, it can also be quite dangerous, especially during high tide or stormy weather. Exercise caution and keep a safe distance from the edge of the well.

Thor's Well
44.27836, -124.11347

**SCAN QR CODE
TO NAVIGATE**

NATURAL LANDMARK

HOBBIT TRAIL

PACIFIC COAST HWY: 600 MI/ 966 KM FLORENCE. OREGON

44.14378, -124.11749

The Hobbit Trail is a scenic hiking trail located near the town of Florence. The trail is named after the fictional hobbits from J.R.R. Tolkien's novels, because the trail winds through a forest of twisted, moss-covered trees that resemble a fantasy world. The trail begins at the Heceta Head Lighthouse State Scenic Viewpoint and follows a half-mile path down to a secluded beach. The trail is relatively easy, although there are some steep sections and stairs to navigate. Along the way, you'll pass through a dense forest of Sitka spruce, western hemlock, and Douglas fir trees, as well as ferns and wildflowers. At the end of the trail, you'll reach Hobbit Beach that is surrounded by rocky cliffs and features stunning views of the Pacific Ocean. The beach is known for its tide pools, where you can see a variety of sea creatures such as starfish, anemones, and crabs. Whether you're a devoted fan of J.R.R. Tolkien's Hobbit series or simply enjoy hiking in beautiful natural settings, the Hobbit Trail in Oregon is a must-visit destination.

Hobbit Beach
91892-91974 Oregon Coast Hwy, Florence, OR 97439

**SCAN QR CODE
TO NAVIGATE**

HECETA HEAD LIGHTHOUSE

PACIFIC COAST HWY: 600 MI/ 966 KM FLORENCE, OREGON

44.13735, -124.12810

Perched atop the 1,000 foot (305 meters) high Heceta Head, the lighthouse is one of the most photographed on the coast. The light atop the 56-foot (17 meters) tower was first illuminated in 1894. Its automated beacon, visible 21 miles (34 kilometers) from land, is rated as the strongest light on the Oregon coast. You can tour the lighthouse, climb to the top, and take in the breathtaking scenery. Additionally, there are several hiking trails in the area that offer further opportunities to explore this beautiful coastal landscape. For a truly breathtaking experience, I highly recommend taking a moment to soak in the stunning coastal scenery from one of the charming wooden benches located in the Heceta Head Lighthouse park. From this vantage point, you'll be able to fully appreciate the rugged natural beauty of the Oregon coast, with its dramatic rocky cliffs, crashing waves, and expansive ocean views. It's the perfect spot to relax and unwind, while immersing yourself in the unparalleled beauty of this picturesque landscape.

Heceta Head Lighthouse
725 Summer St, Florence, OR 97439

**SCAN QR CODE
TO NAVIGATE**

TO VISIT
VISITED

71

ICONIC
PLACE

TOURIST
ATTRACTION

SEA LION CAVES

PACIFIC COAST HWY: 602 MI/ 969 KM FLORENCE, OREGON

44.12181, -124.12685

As you travel along the stunning central Oregon coast, don't miss the chance to explore the incredible Sea Lion Caves. The largest sea cave in the world, this natural wonder is home to a colony of majestic Steller sea lions and offers breathtaking views of the Pacific Ocean. With a paved pathway and elevator for easy access, visitors of all ages can witness these incredible creatures in their natural habitat. The sea lions can often be seen lounging on the rocks near the cave entrance or swimming in the ocean below. The caves were formed over thousands of years by the pounding waves of the Pacific Ocean. No road trip along the Oregon coast is complete without a visit to Sea Lion Caves!

Sea Lion Caves
91560 US-101, Florence, OR 97439

**SCAN QR CODE
TO NAVIGATE**

OREGON DUNES

PACIFIC COAST HWY: 617 MI/ 993 KM DUNES CITY, OREGON
43.92260, -124.11264

We've come across another breathtaking natural landmark on our journey! The Oregon Dunes are a unique and stunning natural wonder stretching 40 miles (64 kilometers) along the coast. The tallest dune in the area, known as "Chief" or "Goliath," is about 500 feet (152 meters) tall. The dunes were formed over thousands of years by the interaction of wind, waves, and tides, and offer a variety of recreational activities for visitors. Popular activities include sandboarding, ATV riding, hiking, and camping. The Oregon Dunes were also used for military training during World War II and the Korean War. If you'd like to explore the beauty of the dunes, I recommend a company called Sand Dunes Frontier, which offers dune buggy rides. I had a lot of fun on my adventure thanks to their experienced guides and well-maintained buggies that ensured both safety and excitement!

Oregon Dunes Day Use Area
81100 US-101, Gardiner, OR 97441

**SCAN QR CODE
TO NAVIGATE**

COOS HISTORY MUSEUM & MARITIME COLLECTION

PACIFIC COAST HWY: 661 MI/ 1064 KM COOS BAY, OREGON

43.37562, -124.21257

Welcome to Coos Bay the largest city on the Oregon coast. The name "Coos" is derived from a Native American tribe that lived in the area, known as the Coos. If you're interested in the history and culture of Coos Bay, I highly recommend paying a visit to the Coos History Museum & Maritime Collection. This fascinating museum offers a unique and engaging look at the area's rich maritime history, as well as the diverse cultural and economic influences that have shaped the region over the years. One of the standout features of the museum is its collection of historic boats and maritime artifacts, which provide a tangible glimpse into the area's seafaring heritage. You can explore a replica of a historic lighthouse, learn about the local fishing industry, and even step aboard a Coast Guard rescue boat. In addition to its maritime exhibits, the museum also offers a range of displays and interactive exhibits that showcase the history and culture of Coos Bay and the surrounding region.

Coos History Museum & Maritime Collection
1210 N Front St, Coos Bay, OR 97420

**SCAN QR CODE
TO NAVIGATE**

BANDON COFFEE CAFE

PACIFIC COAST HWY: 685 MI/ 1102 KM BANDON. OREGON
43.11923, -124.41156

After passing the sign that reads "Welcome to Old Town Bandon" on the right-hand side of the road, you will find a charming small café called "Bandon Coffee Café". This place began in 1995 as RayJen Coffee Roasters, a small espresso bar in Old Town Bandon. By 1997, it had expanded to include a bakery and coffee roaster in its current location. Steve and Margaret Pounder took over the retail café business in 2005, and under their leadership, it grew into a community gathering place. In 2018, Kenny Maddux and Mara Rutherford, former employees of the café, purchased it and have since expanded its food offerings. Mara is a trained baker and Kenny is an experienced barista. Today, the Bandon Coffee Cafe continues to delight customers with its delicious coffee, pastries, and sandwiches, and remains a beloved fixture of the Bandon community. Get yourself a steaming cup of coffee and prepare to explore the charming town of Bandon!

Bandon Coffee Cafe
365 2nd St SE, Bandon, OR 97411

**SCAN QR CODE
TO NAVIGATE**

BANDON HISTORICAL SOCIETY MUSEUM

PACIFIC COAST HWY: 685 MI/ 1102 KM BANDON, OREGON
43.11892, -124.40918

The area that is now Bandon was originally inhabited by the Coquille Indian Tribe, who fished and hunted in the region. The first European settlement in the area was established in the mid-19th century, and Bandon was officially incorporated as a city in 1891. If you want to learn more about the town of Bandon, visit the Bandon Historical Society Museum. The museum is dedicated to preserving and sharing the rich history of Bandon and the surrounding area, and offers visitors the chance to explore exhibits and artifacts. The museum is run by volunteers and open to the public for free, though donations are always appreciated.

Bandon Historical Society Museum
270 Filmore Ave SE, Bandon, OR 97411

**SCAN QR CODE
TO NAVIGATE**

FACE ROCK
STATE SCENIC VIEWPOINT

PACIFIC COAST HWY: 686 MI/ 1104 KM BANDON, OREGON

43.10542, -124.43367

Face Rock State Scenic Viewpoint is a popular coastal lookout located in Bandon. The viewpoint is named after a distinctive rock formation that rises out of the ocean and resembles a human face. According to Native American legend, the face belongs to a woman who was turned to stone by a powerful spirit after she broke a promise. In addition to the natural beauty of the area, Face Rock State Scenic Viewpoint also has a rich history. The beach was a site of importance for the Coquille Indian Tribe, who used it for fishing, hunting, and gathering shellfish. Later, the area was settled by European immigrants who established logging and fishing industries in the region. Today, Face Rock State Scenic Viewpoint is a popular destination for Pacific Coast Highway travelers, offering a chance to appreciate the beauty of the Oregon coast and the rich cultural heritage of the area.

Face Rock State Scenic Viewpoint
Face Rock State Scenic Viewpoint, Bandon, OR 97411

**SCAN QR CODE
TO NAVIGATE**

☐ TO VISIT
☐ VISITED

MUSEUM

SOMETHING AWESOME

PACIFIC COAST HWY: 691 MI/ 1112 KM BANDON, OREGON
43.02632, -124.41493

The stretch of highway between Bandon and Port Orford is known as the Bandon - Port Orford Art Trail, and it's a must-visit destination for anyone interested in art and creativity. As you drive along this scenic route, you'll come across numerous art studios showcasing the works of local artists who specialize in a wide range of mediums, including glass, marble, wood, metal, and clay. One such studio that's definitely worth a stop is "Something Awesome," which is easy to spot thanks to the large wooden figures scattered around the lawn out front. These larger-than-life creations are sure to catch your eye and spark your curiosity. You might encounter an otherworldly alien, a giant foot, or a majestic dragonfly, each crafted with incredible attention to detail and imagination. Visitors to "Something Awesome" can explore the workshop and chat with the talented artists who bring these amazing works to life. So don't miss the chance to experience the Bandon - Port Orford Art Trail and discover the incredible talent of the artists who call this area home.

Something Awesome
47492 Oregon Coast Hwy, Bandon, OR 97411

**SCAN QR CODE
TO NAVIGATE**

HAWTHORNE GALLERY

PACIFIC COAST HWY: 712 MI/ 1146 KM PORT ORFORD. OREGON

42.74339, -124.49343

Inside Hawthorne Gallery in Port Orford, you'd easily forget you're in a small Oregon Coast town mostly known for fishing, lumber, and beautifully rugged shoreline. The modern, sleek gallery space features a stunning collection of abstract paintings in bold, eye-catching colors, while tall, elegant blown glass vessels add to the gallery's sense of sophistication. Large picture windows perfectly frame a range of modern sculptures in mediums such as ceramic, bronze, and hand-forged iron, making for an immersive and visually stunning experience. The Hawthorne Gallery showcases both established and emerging artists, with a focus on Pacific Northwest and West Coast artists. The gallery is a must-visit for art enthusiasts exploring the area between Bandon to Port Orford Art Trail on the southern Oregon coast.

Hawthorne Gallery
517 Jefferson St, Port Orford, OR 97465

**SCAN QR CODE
TO NAVIGATE**

PORT ORFORD
OVERLOOK VIEW POINT

PACIFIC COAST HWY: 712 MI/ 1146 KM PORT ORFORD, OREGON

42.74264, -124.49716

When you're getting ready to leave Port Orford, make sure to set aside some time to appreciate the public art. One spot that's definitely worth checking out is the mosaic tile bulwark and bench located at the ocean view overlook on 5th Street. To get there, simply look for the Ocean View sign that's painted in the middle of Oregon Street – it will point you in the right direction. This place reminds me of Park Guell in Barcelona, Spain, particularly the stunning mosaic benches created by the renowned artist Antoni Gaudi. Take a moment to soak up the beauty of the artwork and enjoy the stunning views.

Port Orford Overlook View Point
475 5th St, Port Orford, OR 97465

**SCAN QR CODE
TO NAVIGATE**

JERRY'S ROGUE JETS

PACIFIC COAST HWY: 739 MI/ 1189 KM GOLD BEACH, OREGON

42.42154, -124.41856

Gold Beach is a small city located at the mouth of the Rogue River. Known for its scenic beauty and outdoor recreational opportunities, it's a popular destination for fishing, boating, hiking, and beachcombing. One of the main attractions in Gold Beach is the Rogue River, renowned for its salmon and steelhead fishing. You can take guided fishing trips or explore the river by kayak or raft. The city is also home to the Jerry's Rogue Jets tour company, which offers scenic boat tours up the Rogue River. Jerry's Rogue Jets was established in 1958 by three brothers: Jerry, Alden, and Court Boice. The boat tours take visitors up the Rogue River a place of scenic beauty and rich wildlife. Visitors can see bald eagles, ospreys, and other birds of prey, as well as deer, otters, and other wildlife along the riverbanks. The tours also pass by the historic Mail Boat Route, which has been in use since 1895 when there was no road access. They are one of the few remaining Mail Boats in the nation and still deliver mail 32 miles (52 km) upriver to Agness, on a daily basis.

Jerry's Rogue Jets
29985 Harbor Way, Gold Beach, OR 97444

**SCAN QR CODE
TO NAVIGATE**

RESTAURANT

PORT HOLE CAFE

PACIFIC COAST HWY: 739 MI/ 1189 KM GOLD BEACH, OREGON
42.42123, -124.41884

The Port Hole Cafe is a popular restaurant located in Gold Beach known for its delicious seafood dishes and friendly service. It has been a local favorite since it first opened in 1982. The restaurant is situated on the waterfront, providing stunning views of the nearby Rogue River. It has a cozy, casual atmosphere, with nautical-themed decor and a comfortable dining area. The menu at the Port Hole Cafe features a wide range of seafood dishes, including fresh fish, crab, and shrimp. The restaurant is also known for its famous, award-winning clam chowder made from a secret family recipe.

Port Hole Cafe
29975 Harbor Way, Gold Beach, OR 97444

**SCAN QR CODE
TO NAVIGATE**

KISSING ROCK

PACIFIC COAST HWY: 741 MI/ 1193 KM GOLD BEACH, OREGON
42.38643, -124.42383

Gold Beach was founded in the early 1850s when miners discovered gold in the sands at the mouth of the Rogue River. The city was first named Ellensburg, but it was changed to Gold Beach in the 1890s. Originally known for gold mining and fishing, in the early 1900s the city began to develop as a tourist destination with visitors coming to enjoy the area's natural beauty and outdoor recreational opportunities. The construction of Highway 101 in the 1920s helped to open up the area to more tourism and paved the way for further development. The Kissing Rock is another noteworthy destination to explore while you're here. There are multiple stories of how the name was given to this rock, but the most common is it was simply a place for lovers to meet and seek shelter from the wind. Or maybe it's that chunk of missing rock that resembles a mouth , but it looks more like a snarl than a romantic expression. You'll absolutely have to decide for yourself!

Kissing Rock
28250-28316 Oregon Coast Hwy, Gold Beach, OR 97444

**SCAN QR CODE
TO NAVIGATE**

ICONIC PLACE

NATURAL LANDMARK

ARCH ROCK STATE PARK

PACIFIC COAST HWY: 756 MI/ 1217 KM BROOKINGS, OREGON

42.20495, -124.37387

Arch Rock State Park is a beautiful state park located halfway between Gold Beach and Brookings. The park is named after the stunning natural arch that stands in the ocean just offshore. The arch is a large and impressive rock formation shaped over millions of years by the constant pounding of ocean waves. Walk along the shoreline and take in the incredible views of the arch and the surrounding coastline. In addition to the arch, Arch Rock State Park offers a variety of hiking trails that wind through the coastal forests and offer breathtaking ocean views. There are several picnic areas in the park, and campsites for visitors who want to stay overnight. This place, as well as the next point of our journey, is part of the Samuel H. Boardman State Scenic Corridor, a breathtakingly beautiful stretch of Oregon coastline named after the first superintendent of Oregon State Parks. The corridor is known for its rugged cliffs, stunning vistas, and unique geological formations.

Arch Rock State Park
22064 Oregon Coast Hwy, Brookings, OR 97415

SCAN QR CODE TO NAVIGATE

ICONIC PLACE

 NATURAL LANDMARK

SECRET BEACH

PACIFIC COAST HWY: 757 MI/ 1218 KM BROOKINGS, OREGON

42.19497, -124.37189

Nestled along the rugged coastline of Oregon, lies a serene and stunning hidden gem - Secret Beach. To get to Secret Beach, you'll need to hike down a steep trail that leads from the small parking lot to the beach. The trail can be challenging, but the views along the way are worth it. Once you reach the beach, you'll be greeted by a wide expanse of sand and surf with towering cliffs rising up on either side. One of the most striking features of Secret Beach is its sea stacks, which are tall, isolated rock formations that jut out of the ocean. These sea stacks provide a dramatic backdrop for photos and are a popular subject for photographers.

Secret Beach
42.19497, -124.37189

SCAN QR CODE
TO NAVIGATE

HARRIS BEACH STATE PARK

PACIFIC COAST HWY: 767 MI/ 1234 KM BROOKINGS, OREGON
42.06752, -124.31120

Brookings is our last stop in Oregon. I suggest you spend some time here at Harris Beach State Park that is situated on a bluff overlooking the Pacific Ocean and features stunning views of the coastline. The park is named after George Harris, Scottish pioneer who settled here in the late 1880s to raise sheep and cattle. Harris Beach State Park offers a wide range of recreational activities, including camping, hiking, beachcombing, fishing, and picnicking. The park has several trails that lead to scenic viewpoints, tide pools, and secluded coves. There are also several picnic areas and a playground for children. The beach at Harris Beach State Park is known for its scenic beauty and unique rock formations. Visitors can explore the tide pools, watch whales and seabirds, or simply relax and enjoy the view. The park also has a campground with sites for tents, RVs, and yurts, as well as hot showers and flush toilets.

Harris Beach State Park
17100 Pacific Heights, Brookings, OR 97415

**SCAN QR CODE
TO NAVIGATE**

PACIFIC COAST HWY

'THE GOLDEN STATE'

CALIFORNIA SPEED LIMITS

RURAL INTERSTATES

URBAN INTERSTATES

OTHER LIMITED ACCESS ROADS

OTHER ROADS

SPEEDS ARE CLEARLY POSTED ALONGSIDE ROADS AND HIGHWAYS ON SIGNS OR DISPLAY PANELS. THE MAXIMUM SPEED LIMIT IN CALIFORNIA IS 70 MPH (113 KM/H). NEAR RESIDENTIAL OR SCHOOL DISTRICTS, THE SPEED LIMIT CAN BE 10-25 MPH.

CALIFORNIA

'THE GOLDEN STATE'
CAPITAL: **SACRAMENTO** LARGEST CITY: **LOS ANGELES**
STATEHOOD: **1850; 31ST STATE** ABBREVIATION: **CA** LENGTH OF
THE PACIFIC COAST HIGHWAY IN THIS STATE : **1001 MI / 1611 KM**
PLACES TO VISIT: **117** ICONIC PLACES TO VISIT: **36** OFF THE
MAIN ROUTE LOCATIONS: **7**

WHERE TO PARK YOUR RV IN CALIFORNIA:

This is a list with recommended RV Parks selected for a safe and comfortable stay:

RV PARKS

Ramblin' Redwoods Campground and RV Park
6701 US-101, Crescent City, CA 95531

Mystic Forest RV Park
15875 US-101, Klamath, CA 95548

Giant Redwoods RV & Cabin Destination
400 Myers Ave, Myers Flat, CA 95554

Bodega Bay RV Park
2001 CA-1, Bodega Bay, CA 94923

Marina Dunes RV Park
3330 Dunes Dr, Marina, CA 93933

Morro Dunes RV Park
1700 Embarcadero, Morro Bay, CA 93442

Santa Barbara Sunrise RV Park
516 S Salinas St, Santa Barbara, CA 93103

Malibu Beach RV Park
25801 E Pacific Coast Hwy, Malibu, CA 90265

Oceanside RV Resort
1510 S Coast Hwy, Oceanside, CA 92054

Circle RV Resort
1835 E Main St, El Cajon, CA 92021

WHERE TO STAY IN CALIFORNIA:

MOTELS

Crescent Beach Motel
1455 U.S. Highway 101 South, Crescent City, CA 95531

Beach House Inn
100 Pudding Creek Road, Fort Bragg, CA 95437

Sea Breeze Motel
100 Rockaway Beach , Pacifica, CA 94044

Stage Coach Lodge
1111 Tenth Street, Monterey, CA 93940

Coast Village Inn
1188 Coast Village Road, Montecito, Santa Barbara, CA 93108

Moonlight Beach Motel
233 2nd Street, Encinitas, CA 92024

HOTELS

Timber Cove Resort
21780 North Coast Highway 1, Jenner, CA 95450

Hotel Caza Fisherman's Wharf
1300 Columbus Ave, Fisherman's Wharf, San Francisco, CA 94133

Hotel Californian
36 State St, Santa Barbara, CA 93101

The Surfrider Hotel
23033 E Pacific Coast Hwy, Malibu, CA 90265

Waldorf Astoria Monarch Beach
1 Monarch Beach Resort N, Dana Point, CA 92629

PACIFIC COAST HWY

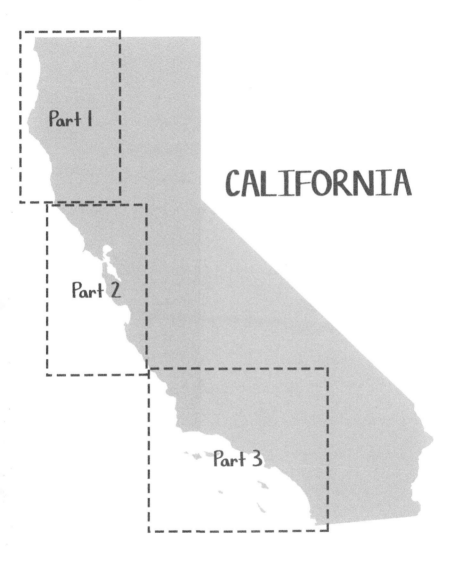

CALIFORNIA

Part 1

Part 2

Part 3

PLACES TO VISIT IN CALIFORNIA (PART 1):

(86) Battery Point Lighthouse and Museum

(87) Jedediah Smith Redwoods ᨊ State Park

(88) Trees of Mystery

(89) Redwood National and State Parks ᨊ ☆

(90) Big Tree Wayside ᨊ

(91) Thomas H. Kuchel Visitor Center

(92) The Larrupin' Cafe

(93) Moonstone Beach

(94) Carson Mansion

(95) Clarke Historical Museum

(96) Humboldt Bay Maritime Museum

(97) Samoa Cookhouse

(98) Avenue of the Giants ☆

(99) Humboldt Redwoods State Park

(100) Legend of Big Foot

(101) One Log House

(102) Confusion Hill

(103) The Peg House

(104) Drive-Thru Tree Park ☆

(105) California Highway 1 ☆

(106) The Westport Whale

(107) Pacific Star Winery

(108) The Pudding Creek Trestle

(109) Glass Beach ☆

(110) Skunk Train

(111) Princess Seafood

(112) Mendocino Coast Botanical Gardens

(113) Point Cabrillo Lighthouse Museum

(114) Russian Gulch Bridge

(115) The Streets of Mendocino

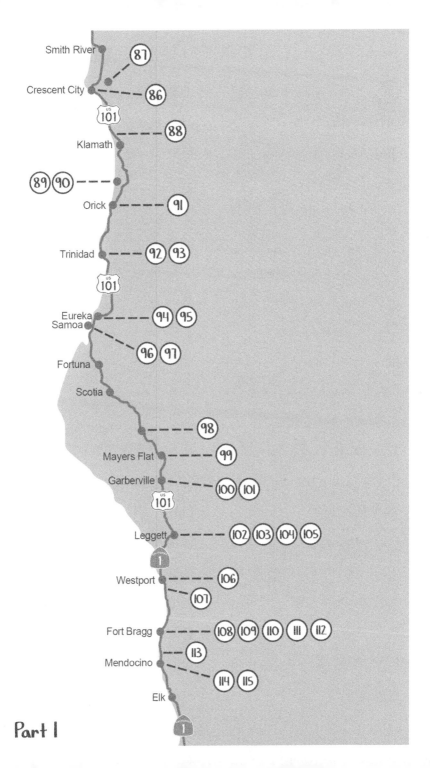

Part 1

PLACES TO VISIT IN CALIFORNIA (PART 2) :

- (116) Point Arena Lighthouse
- (117) Bowling Ball Beach
- (118) Sea Ranch Chapel
- (119) Fort Ross ☆
- (120) Cafe Aquatica
- (121) Goat Rock State Beach Sonoma Coast State Park
- (122) Spud Point Crab Company
- (123) "The Birds" Town 🎬
- (124) Hog Island Oyster Co.
- (125) Bovine Bakery
- (126) Muir Beach Overlook ☆
- (127) Muir Woods 🎬☆
- (128) Golden Gate Bridge ☆
- (129) Palace of Fine Arts
- (130) Pier 39
- (131) Alcatraz ☆
- (132) The Painted Ladies ☆
- (133) Cable Cars ☆
- (134) Devils' Slide
- (135) Mavericks Surfing Zone ☆
- (136) Sam's Chowder House

- (137) Jail Museum
- (138) Pigeon Point Lighthouse
- (139) Shark Fin Cove ☆
- (140) Seymour Marine Discovery Center
- (141) Santa Cruz Surfing Museum
- (142) Santa Cruz Beach Boardwalk ☆
- (143) Santa Cruz Wharf
- (144) Phil's Fish Market & Eatery ☆
- (145) Old Fisherman's Wharf ☆
- (146) Monterey Bay Aquarium
- (147) Lone Cypress
- (148) Point Lobos State Natural Reserve ☆
- (149) Garrapata State Park Bluff Trail
- (150) Bixby Creek Bridge ☆
- (151) Pfeiffer Big Sur State Park
- (152) Nepenthe ☆
- (153) Henry Miller Memorial Library
- (154) COAST Big Sur
- (155) McWay Falls ☆
- (156) Sand Dollar Beach

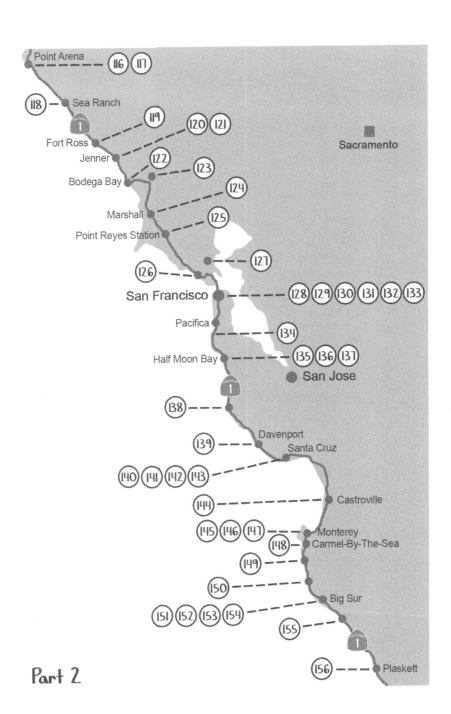

Point Arena 116 117

118 Sea Ranch

119

120 121

Fort Ross

Jenner 122

123

Bodega Bay

124

Marshall 125

Point Reyes Station

127

126

San Francisco 128 129 130 131 132 133

Pacifica

134

Half Moon Bay 135 136 137

San Jose

138

Davenport

139 Santa Cruz

140 141 142 143

144 Castroville

145 146 147 Monterey

148 Carmel-By-The-Sea

149

150

Big Sur

151 152 153 154

155

156 Plaskett

Sacramento

Part 2

PLACES TO VISIT IN CALIFORNIA (PART 3) :

(157) Portal to Big Sur

(158) Elephant Seal Vista Point ☆

(159) Hearst Castle ☆

(160) Morro Rock Beach

(161) Mission San Luis Obispo de Tolosa

(162) Bubblegum Alley

(163) Pismo Beach Pier Plaza

(164) Splash Café ☆

(165) Lompoc Murals

(166) La Purísima Mission State Historic Park

(167) Arroyo Hondo Vista Point

(168) Santa Barbara County Courthouse

(169) Stearns Wharf ☆

(170) Santa Barbara Maritime Museum

(171) Moreton Bay Fig Tree

(172) Ventura Harbor Village

(173) Point Mugu Missile Park

(174) Neptune's Net ☆

(175) El Matador State Beach ☆

(176) Point Dume ☆

(177) Paradise Cove Beach Café

(178) Malibu Pier

(179) Malibu Beach ☆

(180) The Getty Villa ☆

(181) Will Rogers State Beach

(182) Santa Monica Pier ☆

(183) Venice Beach ☆

(184) Los Angeles Downtown ⌂☆

(185) Aquarium of the Pacific

(186) Naple Canals

(187) Huntington Beach ☆

(188) Huntington Beach Surfing Museum

(189) Balboa Island

(190) Inspiration Point

(191) Pirate Tower

(192) Ocean Institute

(193) Casa Romantica

(194) Oceanside Municipal Fishing Pier

(195) Oceanside Museum of Art

(196) Palm Springs ⌂☆

(197) The Flower Fileds

(198) Pannikin Coffee & Tea

(199) SeaWorld San Diego

(200) Balboa Park ☆

(201) USS Midway Museum

(202) Cabrillo National Monument

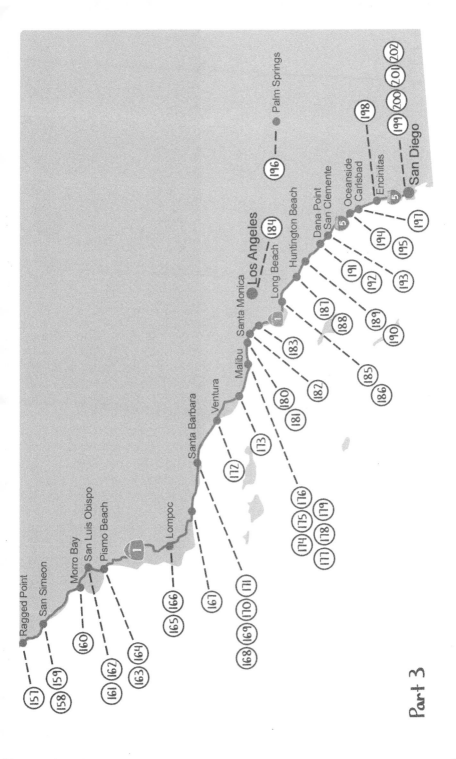

Part 3

HISTORICAL LANDMARK

BATTERY POINT
LIGHTHOUSE AND MUSEUM

PACIFIC COAST HWY: 794 MI/ 1278 KM CRESCENT CITY, CALIFORNIA

41.74533, -124.20159

Welcome to California! The state's nickname is "The Golden State" because of the 1849 California Gold Rush. California is the most populous state in the United States, with over 39 million residents. It is the third-largest state, after Alaska and Texas. Your initial stop in California will be Crescent City, known for its natural beauty, including its rugged coastline and redwood forests. To begin your visit, head over to the Battery Point Lighthouse and Museum. The lighthouse was first built in 1856 and is listed on the National Register of Historic Places. It is located on a small island known as Battery Point, which can only be accessed during low tide by a short isthmus that connects it to the mainland. The lighthouse and museum are open for tours, allowing visitors to learn about the history of the area and the important role that the lighthouse played in guiding ships safely through the treacherous waters of the Pacific Ocean.

Battery Point Lighthouse and Museum
235 Lighthouse Way, Crescent City, CA 95531

**SCAN QR CODE
TO NAVIGATE**

87

 OFF THE MAIN ROUTE

 NATURAL LANDMARK

JEDEDIAH SMITH REDWOODS STATE PARK

DISTANCE FROM U. S. ROUTE 101 · 5 MI / 8 KM HIOUCHI, CA
41.79676, -124.08182

Jedediah Smith Redwoods State Park is a state park located in Del Norte County, California, United States. The park is named after Jedediah Strong Smith, a famous explorer and mountain man who traveled extensively throughout the American West in the early 19th century. The park is home to some of the tallest and most impressive redwood trees in the world, including the Stout Tree, which stands at over 300 feet tall and is estimated to be over 1,000 years old. The park also features a number of hiking trails, including the Simpson-Reed Trail, which takes visitors through a stunning grove of old-growth redwoods. Start your Jedediah Smith Redwoods State Park adventure at the Hiouchi Visitor Center. It is one of several visitor centers in the park and is located in the small town of Hiouchi, just off of Highway 199. The visitor center provides a wealth of information about the park, including its natural history, geology, and cultural significance.

Redwood National & State Park - Hiouchi Visitor Center
1600 US-199, Crescent City, CA 95531

**SCAN QR CODE
TO NAVIGATE**

TREES OF MYSTERY

PACIFIC COAST HWY: 810 MI/ 1304 KM KLAMATH, CALIFORNIA

41.58486, -124.08606

Trees of Mystery is a popular tourist attraction located in the heart of the Redwood National and State Parks. The attraction features a collection of giant redwood trees, a museum, a gift shop, and various hiking trails. One of the main highlights of Trees of Mystery is its SkyTrail gondola ride, which takes visitors on a scenic journey through the towering trees and provides panoramic views of the surrounding forest and coastline. The gondola also stops at a platform called the Cathedral Tree, which is a massive redwood with a hollowed-out center that visitors can walk through. Other attractions at Trees of Mystery include Redwood Canopy Trail. You'll walk aerial netted suspension bridges through majestic old-growth redwoods at mid-canopy level with viewing platforms 50-100 feet (15-30 meters) high in the trees. There are also several hiking trails that wind through the forest and past iconic landmarks such as the Bigfoot and Paul Bunyan statues.

Trees of Mystery
15500 US-101, Klamath, CA 95548

**SCAN QR CODE
TO NAVIGATE**

89

 OFF THE MAIN ROUTE

 NATURAL LANDMARK

 ICONIC PLACE

REDWOOD NATIONAL AND STATE PARKS

DISTANCE FROM U. S. ROUTE 101 : 6 MI / 10 KM ORICK, CA

41.40153, -124.04171

Now it's time to head to the Redwood National and State Parks. These protected areas offer visitors the chance to explore some of the most stunning natural wonders in the world. The parks are renowned for their towering old-growth redwood forests, home to a diverse array of wildlife from Roosevelt elk to black bears and mountain lions. The parks offer a wide range of recreational activities such as hiking, camping, fishing, kayaking, and beach combing. Redwood National and State Parks are not only a place of natural beauty but also hold cultural and ecological significance, recognized as a World Heritage Site and an International Biosphere Reserve. This makes the parks a must-visit destination for nature lovers and anyone who seeks to explore the natural wonders of California.

Redwood National and State Parks
41.40153, -124.04171

SCAN QR CODE TO NAVIGATE

BIG TREE WAYSIDE

DISTANCE FROM U. S. ROUTE 101 : 7 MI / 11 KM ORICK, CA

41.37360, -124.01359

I highly recommend taking a detour and skipping some parts of Highway 101 by choosing the parallel Newton B. Dury Parkway. This scenic route passes through the breathtaking redwood forest and is definitely worth the drive. Along the way, it is also worthwhile to stop at the amazing Big Tree Wayside to take in the stunning natural beauty. A colossal redwood tree, believed to be over 1,500 years old, dominates a paved trail, standing over 300 feet (91 meters) tall and measuring 68 feet (21 meters) in girth.

Big Tree Wayside
Newton B. Drury Scenic Pkwy, Orick, CA 95555

**SCAN QR CODE
TO NAVIGATE**

THOMAS H. KUCHEL VISITOR CENTER

PACIFIC COAST HWY: 837 MI/ 1347 KM ORICK, CALIFORNIA

41.28682, -124.09097

You are in the area of Redwood National and State Parks. Head to the excellent Thomas H. Kuchel Visitor Center located one mile south of Orick. Among the five visitor centers in Redwood National and State Parks, this one is the largest and offers numerous exhibits, a video on redwood ecology, a great bookstore, and access to a sandy beach. The visitor center is named after Thomas H. Kuchel, a former United States Senator who played a key role in the establishment of Redwood National Park.

Thomas H. Kuchel Visitor Center
US-101 & Redwood Hwy, US-101, Orick, CA 95555

**SCAN QR CODE
TO NAVIGATE**

THE LARRUPIN' CAFE

PACIFIC COAST HWY: 857 MI/ 1379 KM TRINIDAD, CALIFORNIA

41.08987, -124.15137

Looking for a place to refuel after exploring the stunning Redwood National and State Parks? Look no further than The Larrupin Cafe. This restaurant, located in the nearby town of Trinidad, is a local favorite and a must-visit destination for foodies. One of the highlights is their fantastic selection of appetizers, perfect for sharing or as a light bite before your main course. But the real star of the show is the local seafood, which is always fresh and prepared to perfection. For those who enjoy oysters, they are a must-try option that's sure to impress. But it's not just the food that makes this restaurant special - the presentation of each dish is truly a work of art, making the entire meal a wonderful experience for all the senses. And of course, no meal is complete without dessert, and this cafe offers a range of tempting options to satisfy your sweet tooth.

The Larrupin' Cafe
1658 Patricks Point Dr, Trinidad, CA 95570

**SCAN QR CODE
TO NAVIGATE**

9 3

NATURAL
LANDMARK

MOONSTONE BEACH

PACIFIC COAST HWY: 859 MI/ 1382 KM TRINIDAD, CALIFORNIA

41.02895, -124.11191

Moonstone Beach is a beautiful beach located close to Trinidad. It is known for picturesque coastline, crystal-clear waters, and unique moonstones that can be found on the beach. The moonstones are actually semi-precious gems that are formed from feldspar minerals, and they get their name from their pearly, iridescent sheen that resembles the moon. The beach features areas of shallow water that are somewhat enclosed and separated from the deeper waters, making it a safe place for young children to splash and play. Additionally, the beach is relatively small and not too crowded, an added bonus for parents looking for a more peaceful and relaxing experience. One of the unique features of Moonstone Beach is a small cave located at the start of the beach that visitors can walk into when the tide allows. This cave adds an extra element of exploration and adventure, and can be a fun activity for children to discover.

Moonstone Beach County Park
41.02895, -124.11191

**SCAN QR CODE
TO NAVIGATE**

HISTORICAL
LANDMARK

CARSON MANSION

PACIFIC COAST HWY: 878 MI/ 1413 KM EUREKA, CALIFORNIA
40.80558, -124.15851

Welcome to Eureka, California, situated on the shore of Humboldt Bay. Eureka is known for its historic downtown, Victorian architecture and natural beauty. The city was founded in the mid-19th century during the California Gold Rush, and many of its historic buildings and homes date back to this era. The downtown area is particularly well-preserved, with many buildings listed on the National Register of Historic Places. If you have the opportunity, I'd highly recommend visiting the Carson Mansion. Built in 1884 by the lumber baron William Carson, the mansion is considered one of the finest examples of Victorian architecture in the United States. The Carson Mansion features ornate exterior and interior details, including intricate wood carvings, stained glass windows, and detailed moldings. Designed by San Franciscans Samuel and Joseph Cather Newsom, these architects designed many notable Victorian buildings across the state. The mansion is now owned by the private Ingomar Club, a private social club. While not open to the public, it can be viewed from the outside.

Carson Mansion
143 M St, Eureka, CA 95501

**SCAN QR CODE
TO NAVIGATE**

CLARKE HISTORICAL MUSEUM

PACIFIC COAST HWY: 878 MI/ 1413 KM EUREKA, CALIFORNIA
40.80363, -124.16763

Eureka has a lot of historic charm, and the Clarke Historical Museum is a must-see attraction while you're here. Take a stroll and head over to the museum. Founded in 1960, the museum is named after the family of Dr. William Carson Clarke, a local physician who was also a collector of historical artifacts. The Clarke Historical Museum has a collection of over 25,000 objects that tell the story of the history and culture of Humboldt County, California. The collection includes Native American artifacts, pioneer and early settler artifacts, photographs, and documents. The museum also has a significant collection of objects related to the logging industry, which was a major part of the local economy in the late 19th and early 20th centuries.

Clarke Historical Museum
240 E St, Eureka, CA 95501

**SCAN QR CODE
TO NAVIGATE**

HUMBOLDT BAY MARITIME MUSEUM

PACIFIC COAST HWY: 878 MI/ 1413 KM SAMOA, CALIFORNIA

40.82012, -124.18156

To get from Eureka to Samoa, you only need to cross the Samoa Bridge. Samoa is a small, charming community located near Eureka. Samoa is known for its beautiful beaches, scenic views, and relaxed atmosphere. Be sure to visit the Humboldt Bay Maritime Museum. The museum was established in the year 1977 by William Zerlang, who was an avid collector of marine artifacts for many years. Humboldt Bay Maritime Museum showcases the rich maritime heritage of the Humboldt Bay region and its importance to the local community. Inside the museum, explore a range of exhibits featuring historic boats, navigational tools, and artifacts from local shipwrecks.

Humboldt Bay Maritime Museum
77 Cookhouse Rd, Samoa, CA 95564

**SCAN QR CODE
TO NAVIGATE**

SAMOA COOKHOUSE

PACIFIC COAST HWY: 878 MI/ 1413 KM SAMOA, CALIFORNIA

40.81974, -124.18174

Just a stone's throw away from the Humboldt Bay Maritime Museum, you'll find the Samoa Cookhouse. This historic eatery has been serving up hearty meals to locals and visitors alike since 1890. Known for its family-style dining, lumber camp atmosphere, and delicious cuisine, it was originally established by the Pacific Lumber Company to provide meals for its lumber workers. At the time, Samoa was a company town, and the Pacific Lumber Company was the largest employer in the area. The company built the cookhouse to feed its workers three meals a day, seven days a week. The cookhouse was designed to be able to feed up to 500 people at a time. The cookhouse opened to the public in the 1960s and serves "lumber camp style", or family style, meals at long communal tables. Be sure to stop by for breakfast, lunch, or dinner and experience a taste of the region's culinary history.

Samoa Cookhouse
908 Vance Ave, Samoa, CA 95564

**SCAN QR CODE
TO NAVIGATE**

AVENUE OF THE GIANTS

PACIFIC COAST HWY: 910 MI/ 1465 KM SCOTIA, CALIFORNIA

40.44130, -124.03128

The Avenue of the Giants is a scenic drive that winds through a section of Humboldt Redwoods State Park in Northern California, USA. It is a 31-mile (50 km) stretch of road that runs parallel to Highway 101 and provides access to some of the largest and most impressive redwood trees in the world. The road is named for the massive redwood trees that line its path, some of which are over 300 feet (91 meters) tall and more than 1,000 years old. Along the Avenue of the Giants, you can stop at several viewpoints and picnic areas to admire the majestic trees and take in the beauty of the forest. Some of the notable attractions along the Avenue of the Giants include the Founders Grove, a group of ancient redwoods that are among the largest in the park, and the Big Tree Area, which features some of the tallest trees in the world.

Avenue of the Giants North Entrance
Jordan Rd, Scotia, CA 95565

**SCAN QR CODE
TO NAVIGATE**

HUMBOLDT REDWOODS STATE PARK

PACIFIC COAST HWY: 924 MI/ 1487 KM MYERS FLAT, CALIFORNIA

40.30849, -123.90821

Follow the Avenue of the Giants to reach the heart of Humboldt Redwoods State Park. The park features numerous hiking trails, campgrounds, picnic areas, and scenic drives, as well as opportunities for fishing, swimming, and kayaking in the nearby Eel River. The Humboldt Redwoods State Park Visitor Center is a great starting point for exploring the park. Located near the park entrance, the center offers a variety of exhibits and displays that showcase the natural and cultural history of the park. Inside the visitor center, you can find interactive exhibits that highlight the park's flora and fauna, geology, and human history. There are also displays featuring Native American artifacts and information about the Wiyot Tribe, who have lived in the area for thousands of years. The visitor center also features a gift shop and bookstore with a variety of souvenirs, books, and other items related to the park's natural and cultural history.

Humboldt Redwoods State Park Visitor Center
Pesula Rd, Myers Flat, CA 95554

**SCAN QR CODE
TO NAVIGATE**

LEGEND OF BIG FOOT

PACIFIC COAST HWY: 951 MI/ 1530 KM GARBERVILLE, CALIFORNIA

40.03431, -123.79325

Bigfoot, also known as Sasquatch, is a mythical creature said to inhabit the forests of North America. According to legend, Bigfoot is a large, hairy, humanoid creature that stands between 7 and 10 feet (2-3 meters) tall and weighs between 500 and 800 pounds (225-360 kg). It is said to have long, powerful arms and broad, flat feet that leave distinct footprints. Bigfoot is known to be shy and reclusive, and is rarely seen by humans. It is said to live in remote areas of the forest. Despite numerous reported sightings and alleged evidence, the existence of Bigfoot remains unproven... Whether or not you believe in Bigfoot, you should definitely visit the "Legend of Bigfoot Gift Shop," an enjoyable pit stop along Highway 101. The gift shop is simply delightful, packed with amusing souvenirs! It's a great place to snap some photos. While you're there, take some time to appreciate the impressive sculptures of Bigfoot.

Legend of Big Foot
2500 US-101, Garberville, CA 95542

**SCAN QR CODE
TO NAVIGATE**

ONE LOG HOUSE

PACIFIC COAST HWY: 953 MI/ 1534 KM GARBERVILLE, CALIFORNIA

40.00993, -123.79005

The Famous One Log House is another unique tourist attraction. In 1946, a remarkable structure was built from a 2,100-year-old redwood tree. It took eight months of labor to hollow out a room that stood 7 feet (2 meters) tall and spanned 32 feet (10 meters) long. Weighing four tons, this impressive section of the tree traveled around the United States with wheels attached to promote California's redwood forests, before finally finding its permanent home in redwood country in 1999. The house has a living room, kitchen, dining area, and bedroom, all carved out of the tree trunk. It also has a small porch and a chimney, and is decorated with period pieces from the 1940s and 1950s. Today, the One Log House is a popular tourist destination, and visitors can tour the inside of the house for a small fee. There's also a gift shop and cafe on site. Don't forget to drop by the cafe to get the entry code for a closer look.

One Log House
705 US-101, Garberville, CA 95542

**SCAN QR CODE
TO NAVIGATE**

102

CONFUSION HILL

PACIFIC COAST HWY: 961 MI/ 1547 KM LEGGETT, CALIFORNIA
39.91894, -123.76494

If you're looking for a place to experience a sense of confusion and disorientation, look no further than Confusion Hill! This a roadside attraction has been perplexing visitors since 1949. The attraction features a number of optical illusions and gravity-defying exhibits that are designed to confuse and disorient. One of the most popular attractions is the Gravity House, a small house that appears to defy the laws of gravity. Inside the Gravity House, visitors will experience a number of optical illusions that make it seem as if the room is tilted or that objects are rolling uphill. Other attractions at Confusion Hill include a maze, a miniature train ride, the "world's tallest free standing redwood chainsaw carving", and a gift shop. So, if you're up for a bit of mind-bending fun, be sure to check out Confusion Hill during your Pacific Coast Highway journey!

Confusion Hill
75001 US-101, Leggett, CA 95585

**SCAN QR CODE
TO NAVIGATE**

THE PEG HOUSE

PACIFIC COAST HWY: 966 MI/ 1555 KM LEGGETT, CALIFORNIA
39.87829, -123.72768

The Peg House is definitely a must see when traveling through the Redwoods in Northern California. Hence the saying, "Never Don't Stop At The Peg House". For those who appreciate the finer things in life, pause your journey and discover the perfect blend of delicious food and live music! Peg House is a historic restaurant that over the years has become a popular stopping point for Highway 101 travelers. The restaurant is housed in a building that was originally constructed as a gas station and general store in the 1920s. There is often curiosity surrounding the origin of the name Peg House, and the answer lies in the construction method. Builders utilized wooden pegs instead of nails to join the timbers, a technique which resulted in the structure becoming a notable landmark along US 101 since its early days.

The Peg House
69501 US-101, Leggett, CA 95585

**SCAN QR CODE
TO NAVIGATE**

ICONIC
PLACE

TOURIST
ATTRACTION

DRIVE-THRU TREE PARK

PACIFIC COAST HWY: 968 MI/ 1558 KM LEGGETT, CALIFORNIA

39.85857, -123.71902

Have you ever heard of the unique experience of driving your car through a tree? Believe it or not, you can make it a reality at Drive-Thru Tree Park! This is one of the most popular tourist attractions in the area. Located in Mendocino County, the park is home to a giant redwood tree that has been carved out to create a tunnel large enough for cars to drive through. Visitors can pay a fee to drive their vehicles through the tree and take photos of this unique experience. The tree itself is estimated to be over 2,000 years old and stands at 315 feet (96 meters) tall, making it an impressive natural wonder. The park is open year-round, and visitors can enjoy the beautiful scenery and explore the surrounding areas. During your journey, you will come across several places where driving through a tree is possible. However, I have decided to choose this particular location because it stands out as the most popular and awe-inspiring.

Drive-Thru Tree Park
67402 Drive Thru Tree Rd, Leggett, CA 95585

**SCAN QR CODE
TO NAVIGATE**

105

ICONIC PLACE   TOURIST ATTRACTION

CALIFORNIA 1

CALIFORNIA HIGHWAY 1

PACIFIC COAST HWY: 968 MI/ 1558 KM LEGGETT, CALIFORNIA
CALIFORNIA HIGHWAY 1: 0 MI/ 0 KM
39.86821, -123.71580

In Leggett, you will find the starting point of California Highway 1, also known as the California State Route 1. The highway is known for its stunning ocean views, winding roads, and picturesque coastal towns. You are advised to drive cautiously and follow all posted speed limits and warning signs. The highway is designated as an All-American Road, the highest designation for a scenic route in the United States. It was constructed over a period of several decades, with the first section opening in 1934 and the final section opening in 1966. The highway has been featured in numerous movies, TV shows, and music videos, including the movies "Basic Instinct" "Bullitt," and "The Graduate." Ready to embark on a journey that will make you feel like a movie star?

California Highway 1
39.86821, -123.71580

**SCAN QR CODE
TO NAVIGATE**

THE WESTPORT WHALE

PACIFIC COAST HWY: 995 MI/ 1601 KM WESTPORT, CALIFORNIA
CALIFORNIA HIGHWAY 1: 27 MI/ 43 KM
39.63925, -123.78513

If you've ever had the chance to journey down Route 66, chances are you've caught a glimpse of the iconic Blue Whale of Catoosa. However, if you find yourself cruising along the Pacific Coast Highway, keep an eye out for the impressive Whale sculpture in Westport. The sculpture was installed as a tribute to the gray whales that migrate along the coast of California each year. Whether you're exploring the heartland of America or enjoying the scenic coastal views of the Pacific, these impressive sculptures are a must-see for any traveler.

The Westport Whale
37060 CA-1, Westport, CA 95488

**SCAN QR CODE
TO NAVIGATE**

107

CALIFORNIA
1

PACIFIC STAR WINERY

PACIFIC COAST HWY: 999 MI/ 1608 KM FORT BRAGG, CALIFORNIA
CALIFORNIA HIGHWAY 1: 31 MI/ 50 KM
39.59202, -123.78363

California is one of the largest wine-producing regions in the world, with a diverse range of wine-growing areas. If you're a wine enthusiast looking for an opportunity to taste California wines, don't miss the chance to visit Pacific Star Winery. The stunning barn built from redwood and stone is nestled into a cliff and protected from the waves by a flat rock bench. This unique location allows for natural wine filtration from the crashing waves and salt deposits on barrels creating dense and viscous wines. Its cellar contains oak barrels and specialty equipment for handcrafted wine making using only the highest quality grapes. Pacific Star Winery is also known for its scenic oceanfront tasting room. You can enjoy wine tastings while taking in the breathtaking views of the Pacific.

Pacific Star Winery
33000 CA-1, Fort Bragg, CA 95437

**SCAN QR CODE
TO NAVIGATE**

108

THE PUDDING CREEK TRESTLE

PACIFIC COAST HWY: 1010 MI/ 1625 KM FORT BRAGG, CALIFORNIA
CALIFORNIA HIGHWAY 1: 42 MI/ 68 KM
39.45839, -123.80768

The Ten Mile Railroad, established in 1915 to transport lumber, required a bridge to cross Pudding Creek. The solution was the Pudding Creek Trestle, which remained in use until 1949. The trestle's dimensions are impressive: it stretches 527 feet (161 meters) in length, rises 44 feet (13,4 meters) above the creek, and is held up by 34 uprights. The road was originally built as a railroad, but later was paved and used by logging trucks. Now it functions as a walking and hiking trail, despite having suffered extensive damage from recent storms. Although many portions of the trail have washed out, the Pudding Creek Trestle was repaired and reopened in 2007.

The Pudding Creek Trestle
Glass Beach Dr, Fort Bragg, CA 95437

**SCAN QR CODE
TO NAVIGATE**

TO VISIT
VISITED

109

ICONIC
PLACE

TOURIST
ATTRACTION

CALIFORNIA
1

GLASS BEACH

PACIFIC COAST HWY: 1011 MI/ 1627 KM FORT BRAGG, CALIFORNIA
CALIFORNIA HIGHWAY 1: 43 MI/ 69 KM
39.45261, -123.81349

Welcome to Fort Bragg! The city was named after the Fort Bragg military post , established in 1857. The fort was named after Captain Braxton Bragg, a Confederate Army officer during the American Civil War. A great place to begin your exploration of Fort Bragg is Glass Beach, known for its abundance of sea glass. The sea glass found on Glass Beach is a result of years of dumping, including glass, by local residents into the ocean. Over time, the pounding waves have broken down and polished the glass, creating the smooth, colorful pieces that now cover the beach. In the 1960s, efforts were made to clean up the beach and stop the dumping, but by that point, the sea glass had become a tourist attraction. In 2002, Glass Beach became part of MacKerricher State Park and visitors are now prohibited from removing any sea glass from the beach. If you're interested in learning more about the history of sea glass and its role in Fort Bragg's past, be sure to visit the Sea Glass Museum, located in the city center.

Glass Beach
W Elm St and Glass Beach Dr, Fort Bragg, CA 95437

**SCAN QR CODE
TO NAVIGATE**

SKUNK TRAIN

PACIFIC COAST HWY: 1011 MI/ 1627 KM FORT BRAGG, CALIFORNIA
CALIFORNIA HIGHWAY 1: 43 MI/ 69 KM
39.44551, -123.80682

The Skunk Train is a historic railroad that operates in Mendocino County. The train runs through the redwood forests of the Noyo River Canyon, providing passengers with scenic views of the rugged terrain and natural beauty of the area. The train was originally built in 1885 to transport logs from the forest to the sawmill. In the 1920s, the train was used to transport passengers and became a popular tourist attraction. The train was named the "Skunk Train" because of the strong odor emitted by the gas engines used to power the train. Today, the Skunk Train operates as a tourist attraction, offering visitors the opportunity to experience the history and natural beauty of the region. The train departs on a variety of excursions, including round-trip rides through the Noyo River Canyon, special events like the Pumpkin Express in the Fall, and holiday-themed rides during the winter season.

The Skunk Train & Rail Bikes
100 W Laurel St, Fort Bragg, CA 95437

**SCAN QR CODE
TO NAVIGATE**

☐ TO VISIT
☐ VISITED

111

PRINCESS SEAFOOD

PACIFIC COAST HWY: 1012 MI/ 1629 KM FORT BRAGG, CALIFORNIA
CALIFORNIA HIGHWAY 1: 44 MI/ 71 KM
39.42784, -123.80553

It's time to indulge in the delicious seafood Fort Bragg is renowned for! The city has numerous seafood restaurants, but I recommend Princess Seafood Restaurant because of their inspiring story. During fishing season, their boat called "Princess" goes out to catch fresh Sablefish and Dungeness Crab with an all-female crew. Their restaurant offers the freshest, most flavorful seafood. Unlike boring fried fish and chips, everything here is grilled to perfection! Located by the picturesque Noyo River and Noyo Bridge, the restaurant features live music on weekends. With mouth-watering food, exceptional service, and a pleasant ocean breeze, what more could you ask for?

Princess Seafood Restaurant
32096 N Harbor Dr, Fort Bragg, CA 95437

**SCAN QR CODE
TO NAVIGATE**

MENDOCINO COAST BOTANICAL GARDENS

PACIFIC COAST HWY: 1013 MI/ 1630 KM FORT BRAGG, CALIFORNIA
CALIFORNIA HIGHWAY 1: 45 MI/ 72 KM
39.40912, -123.80953

Make sure to add a visit to the Mendocino Coast Botanical Gardens to your itinerary before leaving Fort Bragg. This stunning 47-acre garden is a must-see attraction on the Mendocino Coast, with a diverse collection of plants and themed gardens to explore. It is home to a diverse collection of plants from around the world, including rhododendrons, fuchsias, succulents, and many others. Take a self-guided tour through various themed gardens, including the Dahlia Garden, the Perennial Garden, the Heath and Heather Garden, and the Succulent Garden. Whether you're a nature lover, a gardening enthusiast, or just looking for a peaceful place to unwind, the Mendocino Coast Botanical Gardens has something for everyone.

Mendocino Coast Botanical Gardens
18220 CA-1, Fort Bragg, CA 95437

**SCAN QR CODE
TO NAVIGATE**

113

MUSEUM

CALIFORNIA

1

POINT CABRILLO
LIGHTHOUSE MUSEUM

PACIFIC COAST HWY: 1018 MI/ 1638 KM MENDOCINO, CALIFORNIA
CALIFORNIA HIGHWAY 1: 50 MI/ 80 KM
39.35063, -123.81465

Point Cabrillo Lighthouse is a historic lighthouse located on the northern California coast in Mendocino County. The lighthouse was built in 1909 to help ships navigate the treacherous waters off the coast of Mendocino. The lighthouse stands 47 feet (14 m) tall and has a fourth-order Fresnel lens, a type of lens that uses prisms to magnify and focus the light from a lamp. The light from the lens could be seen up to 22 nautical miles (25 mi/41 km) out to sea. Today, a museum is located inside the lighthouse featuring exhibits about the lighthouse's history, details about the keepers lives, and the region's maritime legacy.

Point Cabrillo Lighthouse Museum
13800 Point Cabrillo Dr, Mendocino, CA 95460

**SCAN QR CODE
TO NAVIGATE**

114

CALIFORNIA
1

RUSSIAN GULCH BRIDGE

PACIFIC COAST HWY: 1020 MI/ 1642 KM MENDOCINO, CALIFORNIA
CALIFORNIA HIGHWAY 1: 52 MI/ 84 KM
39.33253, -123.80607

If you're looking for a picturesque and historic spot on the Mendocino Coast, don't miss the Russian Gulch Bridge in Russian Gulch State Park. This beautiful single-arch bridge spans 36 feet (11 meters) across the deep Russian Gulch gorge and was built in 1940 as part of a public works project during the Great Depression. The bridge is listed on the National Register of Historic Places and is a popular attraction in Russian Gulch State Park. The park encompasses 2,320 acres and features a campground, picnic areas, hiking and biking trails, a beach, and a 36-foot (11 meters) waterfall. One of the main attractions of Russian Gulch State Park is the 1.5-mile-long (2,4 km) Fern Canyon Trail, which leads visitors through a dense forest of ferns and redwoods to a stunning waterfall. Another popular hike is the Headlands Trail, which offers spectacular views of the Pacific Ocean and the rugged coastline. For those who prefer biking, the park has several miles of trails that wind through the forest and along the coast.

Russian Gulch Bridge Viewpoint
Russian Gulch State Pk, Mendocino, CA 95460

**SCAN QR CODE
TO NAVIGATE**

115

TOURIST ATTRACTION

CALIFORNIA

1

THE STREETS OF MENDOCINO

PACIFIC COAST HWY: 1021 MI/ 1643 KM   MENDOCINO, CALIFORNIA
CALIFORNIA HIGHWAY 1: 53 MI/ 85 KM
39.30472, -123.79968

Mendocino's town center is a must-see destination for anyone visiting the northern coast of California. Known for its picturesque and charming qualities, the town is situated on the coast of northern California and surrounded by natural beauty, including beaches, forests, and cliffs. Many of the streets in Mendocino are lined with historic buildings and Victorian-era homes, giving the town a quaint and idyllic feel. Take a stroll down Main Street and check out the local shops and galleries, or grab a bite to eat at one of the many delicious restaurants. The town features a long, rich history, with indigenous tribes such as the Pomo people living in the area for thousands of years before European settlement. The first European explorers arrived in the late 18th century, and the county was officially established in 1850. For a fascinating glimpse into the history of Mendocino, head to the Ford House Visitor Center & Museum.

Ford House Visitor Center & Museum
45035 Main St, Mendocino, CA 95460

**SCAN QR CODE
TO NAVIGATE**

☐ TO VISIT
☐ VISITED

116

HISTORICAL LANDMARK

CALIFORNIA **1**

POINT ARENA LIGHTHOUSE

PACIFIC COAST HWY: 1055 MI/ 1698 KM POINT ARENA, CALIFORNIA
CALIFORNIA HIGHWAY 1: 87 MI/ 140 KM
38.95473, -123.74053

Journey onward until you reach the small coastal city of Point Arena. The city hosts various festivals and events throughout the year, including the Wind & Whale Festival, which celebrates the migration of gray whales along the coast. One of the main attractions in Point Arena is the Point Arena Lighthouse, built in 1870 and still in operation today. It is one of the tallest lighthouses on the West Coast, standing at 115 feet (35 m) tall. You can tour the lighthouse and climb to the top for spectacular views of the Pacific Ocean and surrounding coastline. The lighthouse also includes a museum that showcases its history and offers insights into the lives of the lighthouse keepers who once lived there.

Point Arena Lighthouse
45500 Lighthouse Rd, Point Arena, CA 95468

**SCAN QR CODE
TO NAVIGATE**

117

BOWLING BALL BEACH

PACIFIC COAST HWY: 1059 MI/ 1704 KM POINT ARENA, CALIFORNIA
CALIFORNIA HIGHWAY 1: 91 MI/ 146 KM
38.87079, -123.65829

Bowling Ball Beach is a unique and beautiful natural phenomenon. The beach is named after the perfectly round rocks scattered along the coastline that resemble bowling balls. These smooth, spherical rocks are created through a process called concretion, where layers of sedimentary rock slowly accumulate around a central core, forming a hard, compact ball over time. The erosion of the surrounding softer rock layers eventually exposes the concretions, giving them their distinctive appearance. Bowling Ball Beach is accessible only by foot, and you can reach the beach by hiking along a trail from nearby Schooner Gulch State Beach.

Bowling Ball Beach
27520 CA-1, Point Arena, CA 95468

**SCAN QR CODE
TO NAVIGATE**

HISTORICAL
LANDMARK

CALIFORNIA
1

SEA RANCH CHAPEL

PACIFIC COAST HWY: 1074 MI/ 1728 KM SEA RANCH, CALIFORNIA
CALIFORNIA HIGHWAY 1: 106 MI/ 171 KM
38.73347, -123.47730

Need a break during your journey along the Pacific Coast Highway? This is an ideal spot for a quick rest or moment of stillness. The Sea Ranch Chapel is a non-denominational chapel designed by James T. Hubbell, an American artist and architect known for his organic architectural style. The chapel was built in 1985 and is made primarily of wood and glass, with a roof that resembles the wings of a seagull. The design of the chapel is meant to reflect the natural beauty of the surrounding environment, with large windows that provide views of the ocean and forest. The interior of the chapel features hand-crafted woodwork and stained glass windows, also designed by Hubbell. The space is intended to be a place of quiet contemplation and reflection, open to people of all faiths or no faith at all.

Sea Ranch Chapel
40033 CA-1, Sea Ranch, CA 95497

**SCAN QR CODE
TO NAVIGATE**

ICONIC PLACE

HISTORICAL LANDMARK

CALIFORNIA 1

FORT ROSS

PACIFIC COAST HWY: 1096 MI/ 1764 KM FORT ROSS, CALIFORNIA
CALIFORNIA HIGHWAY 1: 128 MI/ 206 KM
38.51426, -123.24356

If you're a history buff, then you simply can't miss visiting Fort Ross on your journey along the Pacific Coast Highway! This fascinating historic site tells the story of a Russian settlement that played an important role in the early history of California, and offers a unique glimpse into the cultural exchange and trade that took place between Russian settlers and local Native American tribes. Fort Ross was founded in 1812 by the Russian-American Company as a trading post and agricultural center, and it served as the southernmost outpost of the Russian Empire in North America. The site of Fort Ross was chosen because of its abundant natural resources, including fur-bearing animals, fish, and timber. The Russian-American Company established a thriving trade with local Native American tribes, exchanging manufactured goods and foodstuffs for otter, seal, and beaver pelts. Today, this National Historic Landmark and California State Historic Park features reconstructed buildings and exhibits.

Fort Ross
19005 Coast Hwy, Jenner, CA 95450

**SCAN QR CODE
TO NAVIGATE**

☐ TO VISIT
☐ VISITED

120

CAFE AQUATICA

PACIFIC COAST HWY: 1107 MI/ 1782 KM   JENNER, CALIFORNIA
CALIFORNIA HIGHWAY 1: 139 MI/ 224 KM
38.44902, -123.11489

Cafe Aquatica is more than just a cafe - it's a home away from home for locals and visitors alike. As you step inside, you'll be greeted by the warm aroma of locally roasted fair trade coffee and the sound of friendly chatter. The cafe is located right on the Pacific Coast Highway, offering stunning views of the ocean and nearby Russian River. It is known for its laid-back atmosphere, friendly staff, and delicious food and drinks. At Cafe Aquatica, the rhythm never stops! Every weekend, you can look forward to live music performances. With a focus on showcasing the best local talent, the cafe has been a hub for music lovers in Sonoma County for over 15 years. Definitely worth checking out!

Cafe Aquatica
10439 CA-1, Jenner, CA 95450

**SCAN QR CODE
TO NAVIGATE**

121

GOAT ROCK BEACH - SONOMA COAST STATE PARK

PACIFIC COAST HWY: 1110 MI/ 1786 KM   JENNER, CALIFORNIA
CALIFORNIA HIGHWAY 1: 142 MI/ 229 KM
38.44081, -123.12642

Prepare to be amazed as you make your way through the picturesque Sonoma Coast State Park. The park features several pristine beaches, including Goat Rock Beach, Shell Beach, and Blind Beach, which are ideal for activities such as swimming, sunbathing, fishing, and surfing. You can also enjoy hiking and wildlife viewing along the park's many coastal trails with breathtaking views of the ocean and the surrounding cliffs and forests. I recommend considering the excellent Goat Rock Beach for your visit. The beach is named after a large rock formation resembling a goat on its north end. Ample parking space is available. This makes it easier for visitors to access and enjoy all the activities it has to offer.

Goat Rock State Beach - Sonoma Coast State Park
State Park Rd, Jenner, CA 95450

**SCAN QR CODE
TO NAVIGATE**

SPUD POINT CRAB COMPANY

PACIFIC COAST HWY: 1118 MI/ 1799 KM BODEGA BAY, CALIFORNIA
CALIFORNIA HIGHWAY 1: 150 MI/ 241 KM
38.32952, -123.05889

Welcome to Bodega Bay! This small costal town is perhaps best known for its fishing industry, a significant part of the town's economy for many years. The town is home to a fishing fleet that catches a variety of seafood, including Dungeness crab, salmon, rockfish, and halibut. Looking for a delicious seafood meal? Look no further than Spud Point Crab Company! Trust me, it's one of the best restaurants in Bodega Bay. The restaurant is located near the Bodega Bay marina where fishermen bring in fresh crab and other seafood daily, ensuring that the restaurant's menu features the freshest ingredients available. The restaurant is a popular spot for lunch or dinner. During peak seasons, there can be long lines. However, I can say that the wait is worth it, as the food is delicious!

Spud Point Crab Company
1910 Westshore Rd, Bodega Bay, CA 94923

**SCAN QR CODE
TO NAVIGATE**

123

OFF THE MAIN ROUTE   HISTORICAL LANDMARK

CALIFORNIA **1**

'THE BIRDS' TOWN

DISTANCE FROM STATE ROUTE 1: 1 MI/ 1.6 KM   BODEGA, CALIFORNIA

38.34597, -122.97179

Bodega Bay and nearby Bodega have been the setting for several films, including Alfred Hitchcock's famous 1963 movie "The Birds." To start your tour of the Hitchcock locations, head to the Tides Wharf Restaurant in Bodega Bay. This waterfront restaurant was featured in several scenes, including the iconic scene where the birds attack the patrons as they attempt to flee the restaurant. From there, take a short detour of about a mile (1,6 km) to the nearby town of Bodega. Here, you can visit two locations used in the film: the Potter Schoolhouse and St. Teresa of Avila. The Potter Schoolhouse was used for the schoolhouse scene where the birds attack the children. St. Teresa of Avila was used as the setting for the climactic scene of the film where the birds launch a full-scale attack on the town. Each destination will give you a unique glimpse into the world of "The Birds" and allow you to experience firsthand the iconic locations that helped make the film a classic.

Potter School House
17110 Bodega Ln, Bodega, CA 94922

SCAN QR CODE TO NAVIGATE

HOG ISLAND OYSTER CO.

PACIFIC COAST HWY: 1140 MI/ 1835 KM MARSHALL, CALIFORNIA
CALIFORNIA HIGHWAY 1: 172 MI/ 277 KM
38.16212, -122.89354

You've arrived at Hog Island Oyster Co., the ultimate destination for oyster lovers! This farm in Marshall is home to some of the finest Pacific oysters you'll ever taste. Come and indulge in our mouth-watering seafood dishes and take in the stunning views of Tomales Bay. Hog Island Oyster Co. was founded in 1983 and has become a popular destination for tourists who come to enjoy the company's fresh oysters and other seafood. Hog Island Oyster Co. also sources oysters from other local farms, as well as seafood such as clams, mussels, and crab. In addition to selling fresh oysters and seafood, Hog Island Oyster Co. also has a restaurant and bar on site where customers can enjoy a variety of dishes made with the company's own oysters and other local ingredients. During the summer months, reserving a place at this restaurant is essential, as it's a popular destination.

Hog Island Oyster Co
20215 Shoreline Hwy, Marshall, CA 94940

**SCAN QR CODE
TO NAVIGATE**

BOVINE BAKERY

PACIFIC COAST HWY: 1150 MI/ 1851 KM   POINT REYES STATION, CALIFORNIA
CALIFORNIA HIGHWAY 1: 182 MI/ 293 KM
38.06834, -122.80650

Welcome to Point Reyes Station known for its natural beauty with rolling hills, farmland, and the nearby Pacific Ocean. The small downtown hosts a handful of restaurants, cafes, and shops. It's also home to the Point Reyes Farmers Market, held on Saturdays during the summer. Don't miss the chance to indulge in some excellent coffee and delicious sweet buns. Bovine Bakery is the perfect spot to stop and treat yourself while strolling through the streets of this charming town. At Bovine Bakery, you'll find a mouth-watering selection of freshly baked pastries, bread, cakes, and other baked goods. Whether you're in the mood for a flaky croissant, a buttery morning bun, or a decadent brownie, you're sure to find something that'll satisfy your sweet tooth. If you're a coffee lover, you'll be pleased to know that Bovine Bakery also serves excellent coffee made from locally roasted beans. So whether you're in the mood for a latte, cappuccino, or just a simple cup of joe, you can count on Bovine Bakery.

Bovine Bakery
11315 CA-1, Point Reyes Station, CA 94956

**SCAN QR CODE
TO NAVIGATE**

126

ICONIC PLACE

NATURAL LANDMARK

CALIFORNIA
1

MUIR BEACH OVERLOOK

PACIFIC COAST HWY: 1171 MI/ 1885 KM MUIR BEACH, CALIFORNIA
CALIFORNIA HIGHWAY 1: 203 MI/ 327 KM
37.86327, -122.58567

A hidden gem lies nestled on the rugged and windswept coastline of Northern California, waiting to take your breath away. Muir Beach Overlook, with its panoramic views of the Pacific Ocean, rolling hills, and rugged coastline, is a must-see destination. As you make your way down the trail, the sound of crashing waves and the fresh ocean breeze will invigorate your senses, and the sight of the cypress grove swaying in the wind will calm your soul. From here, you'll see the beauty of nature in all its glory. The overlook is situated on a bluff about 200 feet (61 meters) above the beach and is accessible via a short trail from the parking area. Muir Beach Overlook is not only a stunning natural wonder but also a site of historical significance. One feature that is not to be missed is the base end fire control station. Unlike traditional gun batteries, soldiers stationed at this site used massive spotting scopes to keep watch over the vast Pacific Ocean horizon for any signs of enemy ships. These stations played a critical role in defending the United States during World War II.

Muir Beach Overlook
Muir Beach Overlook, Muir Beach, CA 94965

**SCAN QR CODE
TO NAVIGATE**

OFF THE MAIN ROUTE

NATURAL LANDMARK

ICONIC PLACE

CALIFORNIA 1

MUIR WOODS

DISTANCE FROM STATE ROUTE 1: 2.6 MI/ 4.2 KM MILL VALLEY, CALIFORNIA

37.89284, -122.57250

John Muir (1838-1914) was a Scottish-American naturalist, author, and environmental philosopher. Muir was a key figure in the American conservation movement and his writings inspired many to appreciate and protect the natural world. In the words of John Muir, "Going to the woods is going home." Let's visit Muir Woods National Monument! The Park is known for its towering coastal redwoods, some of the tallest trees in the world, reaching heights of over 300 feet (91 meters). The monument features a number of trails for visitors to explore, including a wheelchair accessible boardwalk that provides easy access to the towering redwoods. The park is home to a wide variety of plants and animals, including several rare and endangered species. You can also learn about the area's natural history at the park's visitor center, which features exhibits on the ecology and geology of the redwood forest. Due to its popularity and fragile ecosystem, Muir Woods has a number of regulations in place to protect the park's natural resources. Visitors are required to stay on designated trails, and dogs and bicycles are not allowed on the trails.

Muir Woods Visitor Center
1 Muir Woods Rd, Mill Valley, CA 94941

**SCAN QR CODE
TO NAVIGATE**

☐ TO VISIT
☐ VISITED

128

ICONIC
PLACE

HISTORICAL
LANDMARK

CALIFORNIA

1

GOLDEN GATE BRIDGE

PACIFIC COAST HWY: 1183 MI/ 1904 KM SAN FRANCISCO, CALIFORNIA
CALIFORNIA HIGHWAY 1: 215 MI/ 346 KM
37.81996, -122.47855

The Golden Gate Bridge is one of the most iconic landmarks in the United States and a must-see destination for anyone visiting the San Francisco Bay Area. Completed in 1937, this suspension bridge spans 1.7 miles (2,7 km) and connects San Francisco to Marin County. The bridge's orange-red color makes it easily recognizable and provides a stunning contrast against the blue waters of the Pacific Ocean and the green hills of the surrounding landscape. Whether viewed from afar or up close, the Golden Gate Bridge is a magnificent sight to behold. The bridge is one of the most photographed landmarks in the world, with an estimated 10 million people visiting each year and has been featured in numerous films, including "Vertigo," "X-Men: The Last Stand," and "Rise of the Planet of the Apes." For an unparalleled view and the perfect photo opportunity, I highly recommend visiting Battery Spencer. This location offers a stunning panorama of the Golden Gate Bridge and its surrounding scenery, including the San Francisco Bay and the city skyline.

Golden Gate Bridge
Golden Gate Bridge, San Francisco, CA 94129

**SCAN QR CODE
TO NAVIGATE**

129

HISTORICAL LANDMARK

CALIFORNIA 1

PALACE OF FINE ARTS

PACIFIC COAST HWY: 1186 MI/ 1909 KM SAN FRANCISCO, CALIFORNIA
CALIFORNIA HIGHWAY 1: 218 MI/ 351 KM
37.80292, -122.44842

Welcome to San Francisco! It is the fourth most populous city in California. Known for its foggy weather, these atmospheric conditions are caused by the cool ocean air meeting the warmer inland air. Begin your San Francisco adventure by visiting the stunning Palace of Fine Arts. Originally built for the 1915 Panama-Pacific Exposition, this architectural marvel is now a popular attraction for visitors from all over the world. The Palace of Fine Arts features a beautiful Greco-Roman design with a massive dome, Corinthian columns, and a tranquil lagoon that reflects the picturesque structure. The intricate details of the building's exterior, including its ornate friezes and sculptures, are a testament to the artistry and skill of its creators. Inside, the palace houses a theater that hosts a variety of performances, including ballet, theater, and concerts. The surrounding park area is perfect for picnics, strolls, or simply relaxing and enjoying the views of the palace and its surroundings. You can take a leisurely walk around the lagoon, admiring the swans that make the area their home.

Palace of Fine Arts
3601 Lyon St, San Francisco, CA 94123

**SCAN QR CODE
TO NAVIGATE**

CALIFORNIA
1

PIER 39

PACIFIC COAST HWY: 1186 MI/ 1909 KM   SAN FRANCISCO, CALIFORNIA
CALIFORNIA HIGHWAY 1: 218 MI/ 351 KM
37.80867, -122.40982

Pier 39 is a another must-visit destination for travelers to San Francisco. Located on the historic waterfront, this vibrant pier offers breathtaking views of the city skyline, the Golden Gate Bridge, and Alcatraz Island. With a diverse array of shops, restaurants, and attractions, there is something for everyone at Pier 39. One of the highlights of Pier 39 is the famous sea lions. These playful creatures have made the pier their home since 1990 and can often be seen lounging on the docks, barking and sunbathing. You can watch them up close from designated viewing areas or take a narrated harbor cruise for an even closer look. For those looking for a unique shopping experience, Pier 39 has over 80 specialty shops and boutiques, offering everything from handmade jewelry to San Francisco-themed souvenirs. Foodies will love the variety of dining options available, from fresh seafood to classic American fare, as well as the iconic clam chowder served in sourdough bread bowls.

Pier 39
The Embarcadero, San Francisco, CA 94133

**SCAN QR CODE
TO NAVIGATE**

TO VISIT
VISITED

131

CALIFORNIA

1

ALCATRAZ

PACIFIC COAST HWY: 1186 MI/ 1909 KM SAN FRANCISCO, CALIFORNIA
CALIFORNIA HIGHWAY 1: 218 MI/ 351 KM
37.82697, -122.42296

Alcatraz Island is one of the most fascinating and iconic destinations in the United States! This small island located in San Francisco Bay is a place of rich history, intrigue, and natural beauty. From the stunning views of the Bay Area to the notorious prison that once housed some of America's most dangerous criminals, Alcatraz is a must-see destination for anyone interested in American history, crime, or simply seeking a unique and exciting adventure. Alcatraz Island's most famous attraction is, of course, the Alcatraz Federal Penitentiary. Opened in 1934 and closed in 1963, the prison was home to some of America's most notorious criminals, including Al Capone and Robert Stroud. You can tour the cellblocks, see the tiny cells where prisoners lived, and even stand in the "hole", a small, windowless cell used for punishment. You'll hear stories of daring escapes and gruesome deaths, and get a glimpse into the harsh reality of prison life on "The Rock". It's a good idea to book your tickets online in advance.

Alcatraz Island
Alcatraz Island, San Francisco, CA 94133

**SCAN QR CODE
TO NAVIGATE**

132

ICONIC PLACE · HISTORICAL LANDMARK

CALIFORNIA **1**

THE PAINTED LADIES

PACIFIC COAST HWY: 1186 MI/ 1909 KM SAN FRANCISCO, CALIFORNIA
CALIFORNIA HIGHWAY 1: 218 MI/ 351 KM
37.77627, -122.43277

Whether you're a fan of the iconic 90s TV show "Full House" or just appreciate stunning architecture, The Painted Ladies are a can't-miss attraction in San Francisco. This row of six Victorian and Edwardian houses, located at 710-720 Steiner Street in the Alamo Square neighborhood, was built in the late 1800s. The houses are known for their unique and colorful paint job, which highlights their ornate architectural details. They have become an iconic symbol of San Francisco and are often featured in photographs and films that depict the city. The Painted Ladies are also sometimes referred to as "Postcard Row" because of their popularity as a photographic subject. The houses overlook Alamo Square Park, which provides a stunning backdrop for photos. The owners of the Painted Ladies have a strict rule against allowing commercial photo shoots on their properties, but visitors are welcome to take photos of the houses from the public sidewalk or from Alamo Square Park.

The Painted Ladies
Steiner St &, Hayes St, San Francisco, CA 94117

**SCAN QR CODE
TO NAVIGATE**

133

ICONIC PLACE

TOURIST ATTRACTION

CALIFORNIA 1

CABLE CARS

PACIFIC COAST HWY: 1186 MI/ 1909 KM SAN FRANCISCO, CALIFORNIA
CALIFORNIA HIGHWAY 1: 218 MI/ 351 KM
37.79462, -122.41154

Cable cars are a famous and iconic part of San Francisco's transportation system. This cable car system is the world's last manually operated one, and has been in operation since 1873. The cable cars are a fun and unique way to see the city's hills and landmarks, and they offer a nostalgic, timeless experience. The cable car system consists of three lines: the Powell-Mason line, the Powell-Hyde line (the best one), and the California line. Each line has its own unique route and provides access to different parts of the city. Riding a cable car is a great way to see some of San Francisco's most famous landmarks. The cable cars also offer stunning views of the city's hills and architecture. If you're interested in learning more about the history and operation, a visit to the Cable Car Museum is a must. If you plan to ride the cable cars, be prepared for long lines, especially during peak tourist season.

San Francisco Cable Car Museum
1201 Mason St, San Francisco, CA 94108

**SCAN QR CODE
TO NAVIGATE**

CALIFORNIA
1

DEVIL'S SLIDE

PACIFIC COAST HWY: 1202 MI/ 1934 KM PACIFICA, CALIFORNIA
CALIFORNIA HIGHWAY 1: 235 MI/ 378 KM
37.57243, -122.51643

The name "Devil's Slide" refers to a steep, rocky promontory that extends out into the ocean along this stretch of road. In the past, Devil's Slide was considered a dangerous section of the Pacific Coast Highway due to its steep cliffs and sharp curves. In order to make the road safer, a tunnel was constructed beneath the Devil's Slide promontory. The tunnel, known as the Tom Lantos Tunnel, opened in 2013 and is now used by motorists traveling between Pacifica and Montara. Today, Devil's Slide can only be hiked by foot or by bicycle. Also, don't forget to check out The Devil's Bunker. It was constructed during World War II as a crucial part of the city's defense strategy. The bunker's strategic location on top of Devil's Peak made it an ideal vantage point for spotting incoming enemy ships. Today, it's abandoned and graffiti artists have covered it with tags and murals. Notice how the Devil's Peak bunker bears a resemblance to the iconic AT-AT walkers from the Star Wars franchise.

South Parking, Devils' Slide Trail
5981 Devil's Slide Trail, Pacifica, CA 94044

**SCAN QR CODE
TO NAVIGATE**

135

ICONIC PLACE

NATURAL LANDMARK

CALIFORNIA
1

MAVERICKS SURFING ZONE

PACIFIC COAST HWY: 1208 MI/ 1944 KM HALF MOON BAY, CALIFORNIA
CALIFORNIA HIGHWAY 1: 240 MI/ 386 KM
37.49557, -122.49668

The Mavericks Surfing Zone is a well-known big wave surfing spot located in Half Moon Bay. It's named after nearby Maverick's Beach, known for massive waves that can reach up to 60 feet (18 meters) in height. Maverick's Beach is located about half a mile from shore, and the waves are created by a unique combination of underwater rock formations and ocean currents. The waves are so powerful that only experienced big wave surfers are able to ride them. The area is also known for hosting the Mavericks Surf Contest, which takes place when the waves reach their peak size during the winter months. The prestigious contest attracts the best surfers in the world. Due to the extreme conditions, it is important for surfers to have the proper equipment and experience before attempting to surf at the Mavericks Surfing Zone. To set the tone, consider watching the film, "Chasing Mavericks" before you get there!

Mavericks Beach
22 W Point Ave, Half Moon Bay, CA 94038

**SCAN QR CODE
TO NAVIGATE**

SAM'S CHOWDER HOUSE

PACIFIC COAST HWY: 1208 MI/ 1944 KM HALF MOON BAY, CALIFORNIA
CALIFORNIA HIGHWAY 1: 240 MI/ 386 KM
37.50248, -122.47583

Let's fuel up with some seafood! Sam's Chowder House is a popular seafood restaurant located in Half Moon Bay, California. Situated on the scenic coast of the Pacific, Sam's has been recognized as one of the best seafood restaurants in the Bay Area. The restaurant is known for its fresh seafood dishes, including clam chowder, lobster rolls, fish and chips, and crab cakes. The restaurant has a casual and welcoming atmosphere, with indoor and outdoor seating options available. The outdoor seating area offers a stunning view of the ocean and is a popular spot for diners to enjoy their meals. Are you up for trying the local favorite, a nice, hearty bowl of clam chowder?

Sam's Chowder House
4210 CA-1, Half Moon Bay, CA 94019

**SCAN QR CODE
TO NAVIGATE**

HISTORICAL
LANDMARK

CALIFORNIA
1

JAIL MUSEUM

PACIFIC COAST HWY: 1212 MI/ 1951 KM HALF MOON BAY, CALIFORNIA
CALIFORNIA HIGHWAY 1: 244 MI/ 393 KM
37.46324, -122.42822

Half Moon Bay, a charming coastal town in San Mateo County, California, has a fascinating history that is tied to the area's agricultural roots and the California Gold Rush. The town was first inhabited by Ohlone Indians before Spanish missionaries arrived. It was known as San Benito and then Spanishtown before adopting its current name in 1874. Before the Half Moon Bay jail was constructed, lawbreakers were held in a small wooden shed in the backyard of a judge's home, which also served as the town's courthouse. The conditions were so terrible that the local newspaper called for a new jail. In response, the Half Moon Bay Jail was built in 1919 and still stands today as a historical museum. It's easy to see why so many people are drawn to this oddly charming place, which truly looks like it was plucked from a Wes Anderson film.

Half Moon Bay Coastside History Museum
505 Johnston St, Half Moon Bay, CA 94019

**SCAN QR CODE
TO NAVIGATE**

HISTORICAL LANDMARK

CALIFORNIA

1

PIGEON POINT LIGHTHOUSE

PACIFIC COAST HWY: 1233 MI/ 1984 KM PESCADERO, CALIFORNIA
CALIFORNIA HIGHWAY 1: 265 MI/ 426 KM
37.18173, -122.39395

Your upcoming destination is Pigeon Point Light Station State Historic Park, a beautiful and historic site located halfway between Santa Cruz and San Francisco. The park is home to the Pigeon Point Lighthouse, one of the tallest lighthouses in the United States at 115 feet (35 meters) tall. Built in 1871 to guide ships along the rocky coast, the lighthouse has been automated and equipped with a modern light but remains an active navigation aid to this day. The light station includes several historic buildings such as the fog signal building, the oil house, and the barn. Visitors can explore the park's natural beauty amid a variety of local flora and fauna, and enjoy amenities such as hiking trails and picnic areas. The lighthouse is named after Pigeon Point, originally called Whale Point due to the abundance of whales in the area. However, in the mid-19th century, the name was changed to Pigeon Point by sailors to reflect the large flocks of seabirds and pigeons, that nest on the nearby cliffs.

Pigeon Point Light Station State Historic Park
210 Pigeon Point Rd, Pescadero, CA 94060

**SCAN QR CODE
TO NAVIGATE**

139

SHARK FIN COVE

PACIFIC COAST HWY: 1250 MI/ 2012 KM DAVENPORT, CALIFORNIA
CALIFORNIA HIGHWAY 1: 282 MI/ 454 KM
37.00408, -122.18542

If you're passing through Davenport, take a moment to visit Shark Fin Cove. It is a popular beach named after a large rock formation shaped like a shark's fin that juts out of the water right off shore. The cove is a popular spot for surfing, swimming, sunbathing, and exploring the tide pools. The beach is accessible via a short hike down a steep trail from the parking area off Highway 1. The trail can be slippery and rocky, so you should wear sturdy shoes and use caution when descending to the beach. Once on the beach, explore the rocky shoreline and marvel at the natural beauty of the cove and surrounding cliffs. Oh, and make sure to snap a picture!

Shark Fin Cove
37.00408, -122.18542

**SCAN QR CODE
TO NAVIGATE**

140

MUSEUM

CALIFORNIA

1

SEYMOUR MARINE DISCOVERY CENTER

PACIFIC COAST HWY: 1258 MI/ 2025 KM SANTA CRUZ, CALIFORNIA
CALIFORNIA HIGHWAY 1: 290 MI/ 467 KM
36.94932, -122.06500

Hello and welcome to Santa Cruz! Your first stop in this amazing town should definitely be the Seymour Marine Discovery Center. It is affiliated with the University of California, Santa Cruz and is located on the university's Coastal Science Campus. The center features a variety of interactive exhibits that showcase the research being done by UC Santa Cruz scientists and provides information about the marine life found in Monterey Bay and the broader Pacific Ocean. Did you know that one of the world's largest displayed blue whale skeletons can be found here? 'Ms. Blue' is an authentic blue whale skeleton, measuring 87 feet (26,5 meters) in length, and she's quite the sight to behold. The massive skeleton was taken from a 50-year-old female blue whale that washed up at Pigeon Point in San Mateo in 1979 and is now displayed right next to the museum main building.

Seymour Marine Discovery Center
100 McAllister Way, Santa Cruz, CA 95060

**SCAN QR CODE
TO NAVIGATE**

SANTA CRUZ
SURFING MUSEUM

PACIFIC COAST HWY: 1259 MI/ 2026 KM SANTA CRUZ, CALIFORNIA
CALIFORNIA HIGHWAY 1: 291 MI/ 468 KM
36.95147, -122.02672

Santa Cruz is a mecca for surfers, who flock to its shores year-round to catch some waves. Santa Cruz has a rich surfing culture with a long history of hosting surf competitions and producing world-class surfers. The city's iconic surf spots, like Steamer Lane and Pleasure Point, attract surfers from all over the world who come to experience the area's perfect waves and laid-back vibe. If you're interested in exploring the rich surfing culture and history of Santa Cruz, a great starting point is visiting the Santa Cruz Surfing Museum. This museum opened in June 1986 as the first surfing museum in the world. It's located inside the Mark Abbott Memorial Lighthouse at Lighthouse Point and offers a fascinating collection of exhibits and artifacts that trace the evolution of surfing in Santa Cruz and beyond.

Santa Cruz Surfing Museum
701 W Cliff Dr, Santa Cruz, CA 95060

**SCAN QR CODE
TO NAVIGATE**

☐ TO VISIT
☐ VISITED

142

SANTA CRUZ
BEACH BOARDWALK

PACIFIC COAST HWY: 1260 MI/ 2028 KM SANTA CRUZ, CALIFORNIA
CALIFORNIA HIGHWAY 1: 292 MI/ 470 KM
36.96431, -122.01868

Looking for a fun-filled, beachfront adventure? Look no further than the Santa Cruz Beach Boardwalk! This iconic amusement park has been thrilling visitors since 1907. Located on the beachfront, this is one of the oldest surviving amusement parks in California. The Boardwalk features numerous rides and attractions, including a wooden roller coaster, a Ferris wheel, a log flume, and a number of carnival games. In addition to rides and games, the Boardwalk is also home to several restaurants and shops. One of the most popular attractions is the historic Giant Dipper roller coaster, built in 1924 and one of the oldest wooden roller coasters in the world. The Boardwalk also hosts a number of events throughout the year, including free movies on the beach, concerts, and other special events. It is open year-round, but the rides and attractions have seasonal schedules.

Santa Cruz Beach Boardwalk
400 Beach St, Santa Cruz, CA 95060

**SCAN QR CODE
TO NAVIGATE**

143

HISTORICAL
LANDMARK

CALIFORNIA

1

SANTA CRUZ WHARF

PACIFIC COAST HWY: 1260 MI/ 2028 KM SANTA CRUZ, CALIFORNIA
CALIFORNIA HIGHWAY 1: 292 MI/ 470 KM
36.95728, -122.01728

If you're looking for a change of pace after the adrenaline rush of the Giant Dipper, head over to nearby Santa Cruz Wharf. This historic pier is the perfect place to unwind and take in the stunning views of Monterey Bay. The Wharf was originally built in 1914 for shipping lumber and other goods. Today, it's a popular tourist attraction. Santa Cruz Wharf has been featured in several movies and TV shows, including "The Lost Boys," "Sudden Impact," and "Big Little Lies." Take a leisurely stroll along the wooden planks of the pier and stop in at one of the many shops or restaurants. Sample fresh seafood, browse unique local crafts, or simply relax and soak up the California sun. And for the more adventurous, why not try your hand at fishing off the end of the pier? Santa Cruz Wharf is known for its excellent fishing, and you might just catch a big one!

Santa Cruz Wharf
21 Municipal Wharf, Santa Cruz, CA 95060

**SCAN QR CODE
TO NAVIGATE**

TO VISIT
VISITED

144

PHIL'S FISH
MARKET & EATERY

PACIFIC COAST HWY: 1288 MI/ 2060 KM CASTROVILLE, CALIFORNIA
CALIFORNIA HIGHWAY 1: 320 MI/ 515 KM
36.76574, -121.75829

Located halfway between the bustling cities of Santa Cruz and Monterey lies the small town of Castroville. While you're there, be sure to try the famous seafood dishes at Phil's Fish Market & Eatery. The restaurant has gained a reputation for fresh seafood, including locally caught fish and shellfish. Some of the popular dishes at Phil's Fish Market & Eatery include the cioppino, clam chowder, and fish tacos. In addition to its restaurant, Phil's Fish Market & Eatery also operates a fish market where customers can purchase fresh seafood to take home. The market features a wide selection of fish and shellfish, including salmon, halibut, crab, and shrimp. Phil's Fish Market & Eatery has won numerous awards over the years and has been named the best seafood restaurant in the United States by Coastal Living magazine. The restaurant was also featured on several television shows, including *Food Network's Diners, Drive-Ins* and *Dives*.

Phil's Fish Market & Eatery
10700 Merritt St, Castroville, CA 95012

**SCAN QR CODE
TO NAVIGATE**

145

ICONIC PLACE

HISTORICAL LANDMARK

CALIFORNIA 1

OLD FISHERMAN'S WHARF

PACIFIC COAST HWY: 1303 MI/ 2097 KM MONTEREY, CALIFORNIA
CALIFORNIA HIGHWAY 1: 335 MI/ 539 KM
36.60379, -121.89337

Welcome to Monterey! This beautiful coastal city has a rich history that dates back to its original inhabitants, the Rumsen Ohlone tribe. In the 1700s, it became a Spanish colony and later part of Mexico, before becoming part of the United States in 1846. Monterey has a vibrant fishing industry and is steeped in maritime history. The Old Fisherman's Wharf is a must-visit destination where you can explore this history and enjoy some of the freshest seafood dishes around, including clam chowder, seafood cocktails, and fish and chips. This historic fishing wharf has been in operation since the late 1800s and is a hub of activity, with plenty of opportunities for sightseeing, fishing, and shopping for unique souvenirs and gifts. Take a stroll along the bustling boardwalk, watch as fishermen haul in their daily catch, and indulge in some of the best seafood dishes you'll ever taste. Old Fisherman's Wharf is a true gem of Monterey where the sights, sounds, and flavors of the sea come to life.

Old Fisherman's Wharf
1 Old Fisherman's Wharf, Monterey, CA 93940

**SCAN QR CODE
TO NAVIGATE**

146

MONTEREY BAY AQUARIUM

PACIFIC COAST HWY: 1303 MI/ 2097 KM MONTEREY, CALIFORNIA
CALIFORNIA HIGHWAY 1: 335 MI/ 539 KM
36.61826, -121.90179

Another great place to visit in Monterey is Monterey Bay Aquarium. This world-class public aquarium is a top-rated destination for visitors of all ages. At the Monterey Bay Aquarium, you'll have the opportunity to see a wide range of marine life up close. From sea otters and penguins to sharks and sea turtles, there are thousands of creatures to admire and learn about. The aquarium is also home to fascinating exhibits about the ocean's ecology and the importance of ocean conservation. One of the highlights of a visit to the Monterey Bay Aquarium is the chance to see the famous Kelp Forest exhibit. This massive tank is home to a stunning array of fish, including leopard sharks, sardines, and rockfish. You can watch these creatures swim among the kelp, which grows up to two feet per day!

Monterey Bay Aquarium
886 Cannery Row, Monterey, CA 93940

**SCAN QR CODE
TO NAVIGATE**

LONE CYPRESS

PACIFIC COAST HWY: 1306 MI/ 2102 KM   PEBBLE BEACH, CALIFORNIA
CALIFORNIA HIGHWAY 1: 338 MI/ 544 KM
36.56949, -121.96506

The Lone Cypress is a famous landmark located near the scenic road in Pebble Beach, California. It is one of the most photographed trees in North America and has become a symbol of the rugged beauty of the California coastline. The Lone Cypress is a Monterey cypress tree that is estimated to be more than 250 years old. It stands on a rocky outcrop overlooking the Pacific Ocean and has withstood the elements for centuries, including high winds, heavy rains, and salt spray. The tree has become an iconic symbol of California and is a popular destination for tourists visiting the Monterey Peninsula. It has also been featured in numerous photographs, paintings, and even logos for various companies. In recent years, the Lone Cypress has been threatened by environmental factors such as erosion and damage from visitors. As a result, the Pebble Beach Company, which owns the land surrounding the tree, has taken steps to preserve and protect it for future generations to enjoy.

Lone Cypress
3210-3272 17 Mile Dr, Pebble Beach, CA 93953

SCAN QR CODE TO NAVIGATE

POINT LOBOS STATE NATURAL RESERVE

PACIFIC COAST HWY: 1310 MI/ 2108 KM CARMEL-BY-THE-SEA, CALIFORNIA
CALIFORNIA HIGHWAY 1: 342 MI/ 550 KM
36.51591, -121.93824

Point Lobos State Natural Reserve is a breathtaking coastal sanctuary nestled along the Central California coastline. This ecological gem is a haven of serenity, with azure coves, secluded beaches, and verdant forests. Embark on one of the park's hiking trails and discover hidden gems like China Cove and Gibson Beach, where you can witness the unspoiled beauty of California's coastline. Keep your camera ready as sea otters, seals, and a myriad of seabirds often make appearances, adding to the area's allure.

Point Lobos State Natural Reserve
36.51591, -121.93824

**SCAN QR CODE
TO NAVIGATE**

GARRAPATA STATE PARK BLUFF TRAIL

PACIFIC COAST HWY: 1314 MI/ 2115 KM   CARMEL-BY-THE-SEA, CALIFORNIA
CALIFORNIA HIGHWAY 1: 346 MI/ 557 KM
36.45655, -121.92405

Buckle up and prepare to be amazed by the beauty of California's Big Sur Coast, located along the Pacific Coast Highway. This rugged and scenic stretch of coastline offers towering cliffs, sandy beaches, and picturesque redwood forests. Take advantage of the many opportunities to pull over and take in the views at one of the many viewpoints along the way. For an especially memorable experience, be sure to stop at the Garrapata State Park Bluff Trail. The trail is approximately 2.5 miles (4 km) long and is considered moderate in terms of difficulty. It offers stunning views of the Pacific Ocean and the surrounding coastline, as well as the opportunity to see various wildlife, including seabirds and sea lions. After that continue your journey, and be cautious when driving along this stretch of highway, especially during inclement weather.

Garrapata State Park Bluff Trail
36.45655, -121.92405

**SCAN QR CODE
TO NAVIGATE**

150

BIXBY CREEK BRIDGE

PACIFIC COAST HWY: 1320 MI/ 2124 KM MONTEREY, CALIFORNIA
CALIFORNIA HIGHWAY 1: 352 MI/ 566 KM
36.37150, -121.90176

This truly iconic bridge is one of the most famous along the entire Pacific Coast Highway. Bixby Creek Bridge spans Bixby Creek and is situated along the scenic Pacific Coast Highway. It was designed by engineer C. H. Purcell and built in 1932 by the American Bridge Company. At the time of its completion, it was one of the longest concrete arch bridges in the world. The bridge's unique design and picturesque location have made it a popular spot for tourists and photographers alike. Its dramatic arches and stunning views of the rugged coastline and Pacific Ocean have earned it a reputation as one of the most beautiful bridges in the world. In fact, the Bixby Creek Bridge has been featured in numerous movies, television shows, and commercials, further establishing it as an iconic landmark on the Pacific Coast Highway.

Bixby Creek Bridge View Point
27494 Cabrillo Hwy, Monterey, CA 93940

**SCAN QR CODE
TO NAVIGATE**

PFEIFFER BIG SUR STATE PARK

PACIFIC COAST HWY: 1333 MI/ 2145 KM BIG SUR, CALIFORNIA
CALIFORNIA HIGHWAY 1: 365 MI/ 587 KM
36.24758, -121.77901

A visit to Pfeiffer Big Sur State Park is a must for anyone driving through the Big Sur region. The park covers more than 1,000 acres and features a variety of natural attractions, including the Big Sur River, redwood forests, and coastal views. The park is also home to a number of hiking trails, including the popular Pfeiffer Falls Trail, which leads to a waterfall in the heart of the park. In addition to hiking and camping, visitors to Pfeiffer Big Sur State Park can enjoy a range of outdoor activities, such as fishing, swimming, and wildlife watching. The park is also home to the Big Sur Lodge, offering accommodations and a restaurant. The Big Sur Station visitor center serves as an excellent starting point for anyone looking to explore the natural wonders of the region. The center is staffed by knowledgeable rangers and volunteers who can answer questions and provide guidance about the best places to visit in the area.

Pfeiffer Big Sur State Park
Pfeiffer Big Sur Rd, Big Sur, CA 93920

**SCAN QR CODE
TO NAVIGATE**

NEPENTHE

PACIFIC COAST HWY: 1335 MI/ 2148 KM   BIG SUR, CALIFORNIA
CALIFORNIA HIGHWAY 1: 367 MI/ 591 KM
36.22183, -121.75928

Nepenthe is the most popular and famous restaurant in Big Sur. Opened in 1949 by the Fassett family, its name comes from the ancient Greek word "nepenthe," which means a potion that can make you forget your sorrows. Nepenthe is known for its stunning views, relaxed atmosphere, and delicious food, including their signature Ambrosia Burger made with ground beef, bacon, cheese, avocado, and special sauce. They also offer a variety of salads, sandwiches, and other American-style dishes. Nepenthe's outdoor patio provides a perfect vantage point to take in the panoramic views of the Pacific Ocean and the rugged coastline of Big Sur. Visitors can enjoy a cocktail or a meal while watching the sunset, creating a truly memorable experience. During peak season, it can be challenging to secure a reservation or find a table. However, the stunning views and delicious food make the wait worthwhile.

Nepenthe
48510 CA-1, Big Sur, CA 93920

**SCAN QR CODE
TO NAVIGATE**

153

TOURIST ATTRACTION

CALIFORNIA
1

HENRY MILLER MEMORIAL LIBRARY

PACIFIC COAST HWY: 1336 MI/ 2150 KM BIG SUR, CALIFORNIA
CALIFORNIA HIGHWAY 1: 368 MI/ 592 KM
36.22084, -121.75376

Big Sur is also known for its artistic and literary community. Writers such as Jack Kerouac, Henry Miller, and Robinson Jeffers found inspiration in the area's rugged beauty and remote wilderness. The Henry Miller Memorial Library is a non-profit arts center and bookstore. It was founded in 1981 in honor of the writer, who lived in Big Sur for years and wrote some of his most famous works there. The library hosts a variety of cultural events, including concerts, readings, and film screenings, and serves as a meeting place for artists, writers, and musicians from all over the world. It also houses a collection of books, manuscripts, and artwork related to Miller's life and work. The library is set in a beautiful location surrounded by redwood trees and overlooks the Pacific Ocean, making it a popular destination for tourists.

Henry Miller Memorial Library
48603 CA-1, Big Sur, CA 93920

SCAN QR CODE TO NAVIGATE

COAST BIG SUR

PACIFIC COAST HWY: 1339 MI/ 2155 KM BIG SUR. CALIFORNIA
CALIFORNIA HIGHWAY 1: 371 MI/ 597 KM
36.20190, -121.72558

For a delightful coffee break, make sure to visit COAST Big Sur, a stunning location with breathtaking architecture. This beautiful cafe boasts amazing architecture, and even has an art gallery and gift shop inside. The quality of the food is top-notch. Whether you choose to sit outside with views of the Pacific Ocean or inside the building, you'll be surrounded by artistic and rustic vibes. The decor is full of unique features, such as air plant walls, a small waterfall, and wooden sculpted furniture, making for a cozy spot to relax from your travels along the Pacific Coast Highway. In fact, this may just be the best coffee-with-a-view experience you'll ever have!

COAST Big Sur
49901 CA-1, Big Sur, CA 93920

**SCAN QR CODE
TO NAVIGATE**

ICONIC PLACE

 NATURAL LANDMARK

 CALIFORNIA 1

MCWAY FALLS

PACIFIC COAST HWY: 1344 MI/ 2163 KM SLATES HOT SPRINGS, CALIFORNIA
CALIFORNIA HIGHWAY 1: 376 MI/ 605 KM
36.15783, -121.67217

A trip down the Pacific Coast Highway wouldn't be complete without a stop at McWay Falls, where you can witness the power and beauty of nature all in one place. Situated within Julia Pfeiffer Burns State Park, the waterfall drops about 80 feet (24 meters) into a picturesque beach cove, where turquoise waters meet golden sands. McWay Falls is unique in that it falls directly into the ocean, creating a stunning vista not found in many other waterfalls. Access to the cove and beach is prohibited, but visitors can view the falls from an overlook on the side of the highway. The area around McWay Falls is also known for its hiking trails, which offer breathtaking views of the coastline and surrounding landscape.

McWay Falls
36.15783, -121.67217

**SCAN QR CODE
TO NAVIGATE**

SAND DOLLAR BEACH

PACIFIC COAST HWY: 1366 MI/ 2198 KM PLASKETT, CALIFORNIA
CALIFORNIA HIGHWAY 1: 398 MI/ 641 KM
35.92325, -121.46869

Sand Dollar Beach is a beautiful less-crowded beach in Big Sur. It is known for its pristine white sand, turquoise blue water, and breathtaking views of the rugged California coastline. The beach is accessible via a steep trail winding down from Highway 1. The hike can be challenging for some due to the steep terrain. However, the effort is well worth it, as visitors are rewarded with a secluded and peaceful beach perfect for swimming, sunbathing, and exploring. You might think there's a chance to find some buried treasure here, but we're not talking about that kind of dollar. Sand Dollar Beach is named after the sand dollars common to the area. These are a type of echinoderm closely related to sea urchins and starfish. They are round and flat, with a hard, white skeleton-like exoskeleton covered in small, hair-like spines. These creatures can often be found along the shore and in the shallow waters of Sand Dollar Beach or washed up on the beach.

Sand Dollar Beach
35.92325, -121.46869

**SCAN QR CODE
TO NAVIGATE**

157

TOURIST ATTRACTION

CALIFORNIA

1

PORTAL TO BIG SUR

PACIFIC COAST HWY: 1381 MI/ 2223 KM RAGGED POINT, CALIFORNIA
CALIFORNIA HIGHWAY 1: 413 MI/ 665 KM
35.78089, -121.33088

If you're traveling northbound, Ragged Point marks the beginning of your journey along the breathtaking Big Sur coast. However, if you're traveling southbound, Ragged Point marks the end of your unforgettable experience along this magnificent stretch of coastline. Here, at Ragged Point, you'll find a stunning art installation known as the Portal to Big Sur, welcoming you to this extraordinary place. Nestled between the majestic Santa Lucia Mountains and the sparkling Pacific Ocean, Big Sur California is a natural paradise that captivates the hearts of all who visit. This rugged stretch of coastline boasts awe-inspiring views, pristine beaches, and an unparalleled sense of serenity that simply can't be found anywhere else. Whether you're seeking adventure or simply looking to unwind, Big Sur California is the perfect place to escape the hustle and bustle of everyday life and connect with nature in its purest form.

Public Art "Portal to Big Sur"
CA-1, Ragged Point, CA 93452

**SCAN QR CODE
TO NAVIGATE**

158

ELEPHANT SEAL VISTA POINT

PACIFIC COAST HWY: 1392 MI/ 2240 KM SAN SIMEON, CALIFORNIA
CALIFORNIA HIGHWAY 1: 424 MI/ 682 KM
35.66296, -121.25773

Elephant Seal Vista Point is a popular viewing spot located in San Simeon, California. It is situated within the Piedras Blancas elephant seal rookery, home to one of the largest mainland breeding colonies of northern elephant seals in the world. At Elephant Seal Vista Point, you can observe these massive marine mammals as they sunbathe, mate, and give birth on the nearby beaches. The best time to view the elephant seals is during the breeding season, which typically runs from December through March. A must-visit destination for anyone interested in wildlife, nature, or marine mammals, and a great place to take in the stunning natural beauty of the California coastline.

Elephant Seal Vista Point
35.66296, -121.25773

**SCAN QR CODE
TO NAVIGATE**

159

HEARST CASTLE

PACIFIC COAST HWY: 1396 MI/ 2247 KM SAN SIMEON, CALIFORNIA
CALIFORNIA HIGHWAY 1: 428 MI/ 689 KM
39.63925, -123.78513

Hearst Castle is a National Historic Landmark located in San Simeon, California. It was designed by architect Julia Morgan and built between 1919 and 1947 for newspaper magnate William Randolph Hearst. The castle features a mix of Mediterranean Revival, Spanish Colonial Revival, and Gothic Revival architectural styles and is known for its opulence and grandeur. Hearst Castle is situated on a hilltop overlooking the Pacific Ocean and consists of four separate buildings. The outdoor Neptune Pool is a popular attraction, as is the indoor Roman Pool, decorated with 1-inch (2,5 cm) square glass tiles in shades of blue and gold. Hearst Castle was donated to the state of California by the Hearst Corporation in 1957 and is now a popular tourist attraction, offering guided tours of the castle and its grounds. It has also been featured in numerous movies and television shows, including *The Godfather*, Lady Gaga's *G.U.Y.*, and *The Adventures of Rocky and Bullwinkle*. Getting to the Castle requires a tour bus ride and a tour ticket, which can be purchased at the visitor center.

Hearst Castle
750 Hearst Castle Rd, San Simeon, CA 93452

**SCAN QR CODE
TO NAVIGATE**

160

NATURAL LANDMARK

CALIFORNIA 1

MORRO ROCK BEACH

PACIFIC COAST HWY: 1426 MI/ 2295 KM MORRO BAY, CALIFORNIA
CALIFORNIA HIGHWAY 1: 458 MI/ 737 KM
35.37189, -120.86464

In the lovely coastal town of Morro Bay, don't forget to check out the beautiful Morro Rock Beach. This picturesque beach, with its pristine sand and crystal-clear waters, is truly a gem of Central California. As you bask in the warm sunshine, take in the breathtaking views of Morro Rock, an iconic 581-foot (177 meters) volcanic rock that dominates the coastline. Morro Rock Beach is a sandy beach that stretches over a mile, and it's a great spot for activities such as sunbathing, beachcombing, swimming, surfing, and fishing. The beach has several amenities, including restrooms, showers, picnic tables, and BBQ grills. The area surrounding Morro Rock Beach is also popular for hiking and exploring the surrounding natural beauty. Morro Bay State Park, located adjacent to the beach, offers several hiking trails and opportunities for wildlife viewing.

Morro Rock Beach
Coleman Dr, Morro Bay, CA 93442

**SCAN QR CODE
TO NAVIGATE**

CALIFORNIA
1

MISSION SAN LUIS OBISPO DE TOLOSA

PACIFIC COAST HWY: 1438 MI/ 2314 KM SAN LUIS OBISPO, CALIFORNIA
CALIFORNIA HIGHWAY 1: 470 MI/ 756 KM
35.28099, -120.66478

San Luis Obispo has a rich and varied history that dates back thousands of years. The area was originally inhabited by the Chumash people, known for their fishing and seafaring skills. In 1769, Spanish explorer Gaspar de Portolá arrived in the area and established a military outpost, which would later become the city of San Luis Obispo. The city was named after Saint Louis, the Bishop of Toulouse, and was officially founded in 1772 when the Mission San Luis Obispo de Tolosa was established. Today, the Mission San Luis Obispo de Tolosa is a popular tourist destination and a significant historical landmark in the city of San Luis Obispo.

Mission San Luis Obispo de Tolosa 1772
751 Palm St, San Luis Obispo, CA 93401

**SCAN QR CODE
TO NAVIGATE**

CALIFORNIA
1

BUBBLEGUM ALLEY

PACIFIC COAST HWY: 1438 MI/ 2314 KM SAN LUIS OBISPO, CALIFORNIA
CALIFORNIA HIGHWAY 1: 470 MI/ 756 KM
35.27912, -120.66385

San Luis Obispo has also a unique attraction that's unlike any other - Bubblegum Alley! This popular tourist spot is located in the heart of downtown. A must-visit destination for anyone looking for a quirky and offbeat experience. The walls of this alleyway are covered in thousands of pieces of chewed bubble gum, creating a colorful and unusual sight that's sure to make you smile. Before you visit Bubblegum Alley, stop by one of the nearby shops and pick up some bubble gum. Once you arrive, you can add your own contribution to the wall by sticking your chewed gum onto the existing mass. It's a fun and interactive activity that's perfect for kids and adults alike.

Bubblegum Alley
733 Higuera St, San Luis Obispo, CA 93401

**SCAN QR CODE
TO NAVIGATE**

163

TOURIST ATTRACTION

BEACH PIER

CALIFORNIA 1

PISMO BEACH PIER PLAZA

PACIFIC COAST HWY: 1450 MI/ 2334 KM PISMO BEACH, CALIFORNIA
CALIFORNIA HIGHWAY 1: 482 MI/ 776 KM
35.13882, -120.64316

Glad to have you at Pismo Beach! Enjoy the sun, sand, and surf! One of the main draws of Pismo Beach is its beautiful beaches. With over 20 miles of pristine coastline, there's plenty of space for sunbathing, swimming, surfing, and more. Popular beaches include Pismo State Beach, Shell Beach, and Grover Beach, all of which offer stunning views and plenty of recreational opportunities. Pismo Beach Pier Plaza is the bustling heart of Pismo Beach. Located at the base of the town's iconic pier, this lively public space offers stunning ocean views, ample seating, and plenty of opportunities for recreation and relaxation. Be sure to check out the beautiful Pismo Beach sign, a popular spot for taking photos. This iconic sign is located at the entrance to the pier. The Pismo Beach sign is particularly striking during the golden hour, when the warm and radiant light of the setting sun illuminates the surroundings. The sign glows with a vibrant luminescence, creating a truly beautiful sight sure to leave a lasting impression.

Pismo Beach Pier Plaza
100 Pomeroy Ave, Pismo Beach, CA 93449

**SCAN QR CODE
TO NAVIGATE**

164

SPLASH CAFÉ

PACIFIC COAST HWY: 1450 MI/ 2334 KM PISMO BEACH, CALIFORNIA
CALIFORNIA HIGHWAY 1: 482 MI/ 776 KM
35.14014, -120.64241

There's an iconic restaurant located in close proximity to Pismo Beach, a must-visit for foodies. Splash Cafe is known for its award-winning clam chowder, featured in several publications and TV shows. In addition to clam chowder, Splash Cafe also serves a variety of seafood dishes such as fish and chips, seafood pasta, and grilled salmon. They also have a selection of salads, sandwiches, and burgers for those who prefer non-seafood options. The restaurant has a casual, laid-back atmosphere with both indoor and outdoor seating options. It can get quite busy, especially during peak tourist season, so it's a good idea to arrive early or be prepared to wait for a table.

Splash Café
197 Pomeroy Ave, Pismo Beach, CA 93449

**SCAN QR CODE
TO NAVIGATE**

165

CALIFORNIA

1

LOMPOC MURALS

PACIFIC COAST HWY: 1497 MI/ 2409 KM LOMPOC, CALIFORNIA
CALIFORNIA HIGHWAY 1: 529 MI/ 851 KM
34.63754, -120.45799

Lompoc is home to a number of beautiful murals throughout the city. Many of these depict local history, natural beauty, and cultural traditions. Here are a few notable examples: Murals by the Lompoc Mural Society: The Lompoc Mural Society has created over 40 murals since it was founded in 1988. These are located on the sides of buildings and depict a variety of subjects, including historical events, landscapes, and cultural traditions. The Wine Mural: Located on the side of a building on South H Street, the Wine Mural depicts the history of winemaking in the Lompoc Valley. The Lompoc Flower Festival Mural: This colorful mural is located on the side of the old Lompoc Theater and depicts the annual Lompoc Flower Festival. The festival has been held in Lompoc since 1952. The Chumash Mural: Located on the side of a building on East Ocean Avenue, the Chumash Mural depicts the history and culture of the Chumash people, who lived in the Lompoc Valley for thousands of years before European settlers arrived.

Lompoc Murals
137 S H St, Lompoc, CA 93436

**SCAN QR CODE
TO NAVIGATE**

TO VISIT
VISITED

166

LA PURÍSIMA MISSION STATE HISTORIC PARK

PACIFIC COAST HWY: 1497 MI/ 2409 KM LOMPOC, CALIFORNIA
CALIFORNIA HIGHWAY 1: 529 MI/ 851 KM
34.66976, -120.42062

To delve deeper into Lompoc's fascinating past, be sure to add La Purísima Mission State Historic Park to your itinerary. It is a reconstruction of the original La Purísima Mission, founded in 1787 by the Spanish Franciscans. The mission was one of 21 established in California during the Spanish colonial period, and played an important role in the history and development of the region. Today, the park offers visitors a chance to step back in time and experience life as it was during the mission period. The park features a range of historic buildings, including a church, barracks, blacksmith shop, and more. You can take guided tours of the park, watch demonstrations of traditional crafts and trades, and even participate in hands-on activities like adobe brickmaking.

La Purísima Mission State Historic Park
2295 Purisima Rd, Lompoc, CA 93436

**SCAN QR CODE
TO NAVIGATE**

ARROYO HONDO VISTA POINT

PACIFIC COAST HWY: 1524 MI/ 2453 KM GOLETA, CALIFORNIA
CALIFORNIA HIGHWAY 1: 556 MI/ 895 KM
34.47403, -120.13807

Arroyo Hondo Vista Point is a scenic overlook situated in Santa Barbara County, approximately 10 miles north of Santa Barbara and just south of Gaviota State Park. The vista point provides stunning views of the Pacific Ocean and the surrounding coastline. Take a stroll across the currently unused Arroyo Hondo Bridge. Built in 1918, it was the first complex bridge built by the California Highway Commission, the agency prior to Caltrans. It served both directions of US 101 until 1950 when the highway was expanded, then was reserved for southbound traffic only. It was bypassed in 1984, but Caltrans wisely recognized its historical value and left it in place. It now serves as a scenic overlook. If you forgot to bring your binoculars, no worries! Use the recently installed telescope and binoculars to scan the ocean for migrating whales and other distant objects.

Arroyo Hondo Vista Point
15550 El Camino Real, Goleta, CA 93117

**SCAN QR CODE
TO NAVIGATE**

HISTORICAL
LANDMARK

CALIFORNIA

1

SANTA BARBARA
COUNTY COURTHOUSE

PACIFIC COAST HWY: 1551 MI/ 2496 KM   SANTA BARBARA, CALIFORNIA
CALIFORNIA HIGHWAY 1: 583 MI/ 938 KM
34.42422, -119.70234

Welcome to Santa Barbara, sometimes referred to as the "American Riviera" because of its Mediterranean climate and oceanfront location. We'll begin our sightseeing tour by exploring the city's stunning architectural landmarks. One such must-see attraction is the Santa Barbara County Courthouse and its breathtaking gardens. It was completed in 1929 and serves as the county's main courthouse. The building is renowned for its beautiful Spanish-Moorish architecture and is a popular tourist attraction. The courthouse is home to various government offices, including courtrooms, judges' chambers, and the office of the Clerk of the Superior Court. Some of the courthouse's notable features include a 360-degree panoramic view of Santa Barbara from the clock tower, beautiful murals, ornate tiles and woodwork, and a sunken garden with a fountain.

Santa Barbara County Courthouse Gardens
1100 Anacapa St, Santa Barbara, CA 93101

**SCAN QR CODE
TO NAVIGATE**

TO VISIT
VISITED

169

ICONIC
PLACE

HISTORICAL
LANDMARK

CALIFORNIA
1

STEARNS WHARF

PACIFIC COAST HWY: 1551 MI/ 2496 KM SANTA BARBARA, CALIFORNIA
CALIFORNIA HIGHWAY 1: 583 MI/ 938 KM
34.41000, -119.68597

After admiring some great architecture, let's head over to the Santa Barbara Coast. Fun fact: Santa Barbara is credited as the birthplace of modern surfing. Hawaiian surfer George Freeth rode the first known surfboard there in 1885. To enjoy the stunning coastal view of Santa Barbara, take a stroll along Stearns Wharf. It was built in 1872 by local lumberman John P. Stearns, and at the time was the longest deep-water pier between San Pedro and San Francisco. The wharf has since been rebuilt and renovated several times, and is now a popular tourist destination with shops, restaurants, and an aquarium. In the 1920s, Stearns Wharf was a popular spot for rum runners during Prohibition. Boats would dock at the wharf and unload illegal alcohol, which would then be transported by car to speakeasies and hidden locations throughout Santa Barbara.

Stearns Wharf
217 Stearns Wharf, Santa Barbara, CA 93101

**SCAN QR CODE
TO NAVIGATE**

SANTA BARBARA
MARITIME MUSEUM

PACIFIC COAST HWY: 1551 MI/ 2496 KM   SANTA BARBARA, CALIFORNIA
CALIFORNIA HIGHWAY 1: 583 MI/ 938 KM
34.40408, -119.69373

The Santa Barbara Maritime Museum is one of the best maritime museums along the whole Pacific Coast Highway, and I highly recommend a visit. The museum's impressive collection and exhibits are sure to fascinate any maritime enthusiast. Don't miss the chance to explore the rich maritime history of the area and learn about the role of the ocean in shaping the local culture and economy. Trust me, you won't regret making a stop at this exceptional museum.

Santa Barbara Maritime Museum
113 Harbor Way STE 190, Santa Barbara, CA 93109

**SCAN QR CODE
TO NAVIGATE**

171

MORETON BAY FIG TREE

PACIFIC COAST HWY: 1551 MI/ 2496 KM SANTA BARBARA, CALIFORNIA
CALIFORNIA HIGHWAY 1: 583 MI/ 938 KM
34.41376, -119.69404

The final destination on your tour of Santa Barbara will be the Moreton Bay Fig Tree. The tree is over 140 years old and is one of the largest Moreton Bay Fig Trees in the United States, with a canopy that covers over 17,000 square feet. The history of the Moreton Bay Fig Tree in Santa Barbara dates back to 1876, when a local businessman named James William Osgood imported four small Moreton Bay Fig Tree seedlings from Australia and planted them in various locations around Santa Barbara. One of the seedlings was planted in what is now known as the Plaza de la Guerra, a historic public square downtown. Over time, this Moreton Bay Fig Tree grew to become a beloved landmark, with its sprawling canopy providing shade and shelter to visitors and locals alike. In the early 1900s, the tree's branches were used as a natural archway for the local electric streetcar line, and the tree itself has been featured in many films and TV shows.

Moreton Bay Fig Tree
Chapala St & Montecito Street, Santa Barbara, CA 93101

**SCAN QR CODE
TO NAVIGATE**

CALIFORNIA

1

VENTURA HARBOR VILLAGE

PACIFIC COAST HWY: 1580 MI/ 2543 KM VENTURA, CALIFORNIA
CALIFORNIA HIGHWAY 1: 612 MI/ 985 KM
34.24099, -119.26555

Ventura Harbor Village is a waterfront shopping, dining, and entertainment destination located in Ventura, California. The village is situated in Ventura Harbor, a thriving marina that serves as a hub for fishing boats, yachts, and other vessels. The village features over 30 unique boutiques, galleries, and specialty shops that offer a variety of items, including beachwear, jewelry, art, and souvenirs. Visitors can also enjoy a variety of dining options, ranging from seafood to Italian cuisine, and a selection of cafes and coffee shops. In addition to shopping and dining, Ventura Harbor Village hosts events throughout the year, including live music, art shows, wine tastings, and holiday celebrations. There are also several water activities available, such as boat tours, kayaking, and paddleboarding.

Ventura Harbor Village
1583 Spinnaker Dr, Ventura, CA 93001

**SCAN QR CODE
TO NAVIGATE**

173

TOURIST
ATTRACTION

CALIFORNIA
1

POINT MUGU MISSILE PARK

PACIFIC COAST HWY: 1596 MI/ 2569 KM PORT HUENEME. CALIFORNIA
CALIFORNIA HIGHWAY 1: 628 MI/ 1011 KM
34.13213, -119.10070

If you're into military stuff, our next stop should pique your interest. But even though it's not the usual tourist attraction, it's worth a short visit! Point Mugu Missile Park features an impressive collection of missiles, including the AIM-7 Sparrow, the AIM-9 Sidewinder, the AGM-65 Maverick, and the Tomahawk missile. There are also several aircraft on display, such as the F-4 Phantom, the F-14 Tomcat, and the A-4 Skyhawk. Point Mugu Missile Park is an excellent destination for anyone interested in military history and technology, and offers a unique opportunity to see these impressive weapons up close. It's worth mentioning that the nearby Naval Base is used as a test and evaluation center for various military aircraft, weapons, and systems. The base is home to the Naval Air Warfare Center Weapons Division, responsible for researching, developing, testing, and evaluating weapons and weapons systems for the Navy and Marine Corps.

Point Mugu Missile Park
10A Naval Air Rd, Port Hueneme, CA 93041

**SCAN QR CODE
TO NAVIGATE**

ICONIC PLACE   RESTAURANT

CALIFORNIA
1

☐ TO VISIT
☐ VISITED

NEPTUNE'S NET

PACIFIC COAST HWY: 1606 MI/ 2585 KM MALIBU, CALIFORNIA
CALIFORNIA HIGHWAY 1: 638 MI/ 1027 KM
34.05318, -118.96246

Neptune's Net is a very popular and famous seafood restaurant located on California Highway 1. It was founded in 1956 by Eastman Jacobs, a retired NASA aerodynamicist. Jacobs was inspired to start the restaurant after spending years studying the aerodynamics of flight and realizing that the same principles could be applied to the design of a restaurant capable of withstanding the strong ocean winds in Malibu. Since its founding, Neptune's Net has become an iconic landmark in the Malibu area. It has been featured in numerous films and TV shows, and has attracted visitors from all over the world who come to enjoy the fresh seafood, ocean views, and relaxed beach vibe. The restaurant offers a variety of menu items, including classic seafood dishes like fish and chips, clam chowder, and lobster rolls, as well as burgers, sandwiches, and salads. The restaurant has indoor and outdoor seating with stunning views of the ocean, making it a great spot for a casual meal or a special occasion. Despite its popularity and longevity, Neptune's Net has remained true to its roots as a family-owned and operated business.

Neptune's Net
42505 CA-1, Malibu, CA 90265

**SCAN QR CODE
TO NAVIGATE**

ICONIC
PLACE

NATURAL
LANDMARK

CALIFORNIA
1

EL MATADOR STATE BEACH

PACIFIC COAST HWY: 1611 MI/ 2593 KM MALIBU, CALIFORNIA
CALIFORNIA HIGHWAY 1: 643 MI/ 1035 KM
34.03803, -118.87467

El Matador State Beach is an amazingly beautiful beach known for its rocky cliffs, clear blue waters, and stunning sunsets. The beach is a popular destination for tourists and locals alike, especially for photography and romantic walks. One of the most striking features of El Matador State Beach is the rock arches found along the shoreline. These arches are natural formations created over millions of years by the erosion of the sandstone cliffs. El Matador State Beach is one of three beaches within Robert H. Meyer Memorial State Beach. The other two are La Piedra State Beach and El Pescador State Beach. Together, these beaches provide a stretch of nearly two miles of pristine coastline. Visitors to El Matador State Beach can enjoy a variety of activities, including swimming, surfing, and sunbathing. However, it is important to note that the beach has steep cliffs and rocky outcroppings, which can be challenging to navigate.

El Matador State Beach
32350 E Pacific Coast Hwy, Malibu, CA 90265

**SCAN QR CODE
TO NAVIGATE**

176

CALIFORNIA
1

POINT DUME

PACIFIC COAST HWY: 1617 MI/ 2602 KM MALIBU, CALIFORNIA
CALIFORNIA HIGHWAY 1: 649 MI/ 1044 KM
34.00120, -118.80640

Point Dume is a stunning natural wonder that captivates the senses and inspires the soul. As you approach Point Dume, you'll be struck by the raw power of the ocean as it crashes against the shore. The sound of the waves fills the air, creating a soothing soundtrack that calms the mind and invigorates the spirit. The sea breeze is refreshing, carrying the scent of salt and seaweed, and stirring the senses. Looking out across the endless expanse of blue, you'll feel a sense of awe and wonder at the majesty of the natural world. This breathtaking promontory sits proudly on the coast of Malibu, California, jutting out into the glittering waters of the Pacific Ocean. From its rugged cliffs to its shimmering sands, Point Dume is a paradise for those seeking to escape the hustle and bustle of daily life and immerse themselves in the beauty of nature.

Point Dume
Cliffside Dr &, Birdview Ave, Malibu, CA 90265

**SCAN QR CODE
TO NAVIGATE**

177

PARADISE COVE BEACH CAFÉ

PACIFIC COAST HWY: 1618 MI/ 2604 KM MALIBU, CALIFORNIA
CALIFORNIA HIGHWAY 1: 650 MI/ 1046 KM
34.02023, -118.78718

Welcome to the city of Malibu, known for its beautiful beaches, rugged mountains, and celebrity homes. The city is situated along a 21-mile (34 km) strip of coastline on the Pacific Ocean. Before you start exploring Malibu, I recommend visiting the Paradise Cove Beach Café. You can lounge on one of their beach beds with an umbrella, order a drink, and enjoy the sun and the views. It's the perfect spot to chill and sunbathe for a while. The restaurant is situated on the beautiful Paradise Cove Beach, offering stunning views of the Pacific Ocean. It serves American cuisine, including seafood, burgers, salads, and sandwiches. They also have a full bar with a variety of cocktails, beers, and wines. The outdoor seating area is spacious and offers a relaxed and casual dining experience.

Paradise Cove Beach Café
28128 E Pacific Coast Hwy, Malibu, CA 90265

**SCAN QR CODE
TO NAVIGATE**

MALIBU PIER

PACIFIC COAST HWY: 1623 MI/ 2612 KM MALIBU, CALIFORNIA
CALIFORNIA HIGHWAY 1: 655 MI/ 1054 KM
34.03651, -118.67617

The original Malibu Pier was built in 1905 and was 700 feet long. It was used as a wharf for shipping and transportation purposes. The pier was rebuilt in 1934 after being destroyed by a storm. The new pier was extended to its current length of 780 feet (238 meters). Today it is a popular tourist destination and a great spot for fishing, sightseeing, and enjoying the ocean views. The pier features several restaurants, including the Malibu Farm Pier Cafe, a seafood restaurant, and a cafe. The Malibu Pier has been used as a filming location for several movies and TV shows, including Baywatch, The O.C., and Iron Man.

Malibu Pier
23000 CA-1, Malibu, CA 90265

**SCAN QR CODE
TO NAVIGATE**

ICONIC PLACE   NATURAL LANDMARK

CALIFORNIA
1

MALIBU BEACH

PACIFIC COAST HWY: 1624 MI/ 2614 KM MALIBU, CALIFORNIA
CALIFORNIA HIGHWAY 1: 656 MI/ 1056 KM
34.03852, -118.65693

If you want to get in the right mindset for Malibu Beach, give "Malibu" by Miley Cyrus a listen. This 2017 pop hit song is a tribute to the singer's time spent in Malibu with her fiancé, and the lyrics perfectly capture the beauty of the city's beaches and the happiness of being in love. After listening, head to Malibu Beach and experience it for yourself! Malibu is known for its stunning beachfront properties and distinctive architecture. The city is also known for its strict development codes, which aim to preserve the natural beauty of the area and prevent overbuilding. Many of the houses in Malibu are located on the beach or have views of the ocean, making them some of the most sought-after real estate in the world. The architecture of these houses varies, but they often feature sleek and modern designs, with large windows and open living spaces. Some of the celebrities who own houses here are: Leonardo DiCaprio, Cindy Crawford, Jennifer Aniston, Pierce Brosnan, Courteney Cox, Ellen DeGeneres, Robert Downey Jr., and Charlize Theron.

Malibu Beach
22126 CA-1, Malibu, CA 90265

**SCAN QR CODE
TO NAVIGATE**

TO VISIT
VISITED

180

ICONIC
PLACE

MUSEUM

CALIFORNIA
1

THE GETTY VILLA

PACIFIC COAST HWY: 1630 MI/ 2623 KM   PACIFIC PALISADES, CALIFORNIA
CALIFORNIA HIGHWAY 1: 662 MI/ 1065 KM
34.04589, -118.56486

The Getty Villa is a stunning museum nestled in the hills of the Pacific Palisades. It was designed to resemble an ancient Roman villa, complete with tranquil gardens, fountains, and mosaics. The museum's architecture and landscaping create a serene and calming atmosphere that transports visitors back in time. As you stroll through the galleries, you'll encounter sculptures, paintings, and decorative arts from ancient Greece and Rome, as well as from Etruscan and other Mediterranean cultures. One of the most impressive collections in the Getty Villa is its ancient Roman sculptures. While the Getty Villa is undoubtedly a place of great cultural significance and artistic value, it's also a visually stunning destination that offers plenty of opportunities for capturing memorable photos and to share on social media. The museum's architecture and gardens are exquisitely designed and provide a picturesque backdrop. The reflecting pool, fountains, and mosaics also make for striking photo subjects. Instagrammers don't skip that place!

The Getty Villa
17985 E Pacific Coast Hwy, Pacific Palisades, CA 90272

**SCAN QR CODE
TO NAVIGATE**

NATURAL LANDMARK

CALIFORNIA 1

WILL ROGERS STATE BEACH

PACIFIC COAST HWY: 1632 MI/ 2626 KM   PACIFIC PALISADES, CALIFORNIA
CALIFORNIA HIGHWAY 1: 664 MI/ 1069 KM
34.03564, -118.53591

Imagine you are in the 90s, with David Hasselhoff and Pamela Anderson running on this beach, while Jimi Jamison's hit, "I'm Always Here" plays in the background. Yes, this is the beach where many scenes of Baywatch were filmed! Will Rogers State Beach is known for its scenic beauty, clean water, and a wide variety of recreational activities such as swimming, surfing, volleyball, and picnicking. It's named after Will Rogers, a famous American actor and humorist, who used to own a ranch in the area. To make your visit complete, don't forget to take a picture with the lifeguard tower!

Will Rogers State Beach
17000 CA-1, Pacific Palisades, CA 90272

**SCAN QR CODE
TO NAVIGATE**

182

ICONIC
PLACE

TOURIST
ATTRACTION

CALIFORNIA
1

SANTA MONICA PIER

PACIFIC COAST HWY: 1635 MI/ 2631 KM   SANTA MONICA, CALIFORNIA
CALIFORNIA HIGHWAY 1: 667 MI/ 1074 KM
34.00830, -118.49875

Santa Monica Pier is one of the most iconic landmarks in Southern California, drawing millions of visitors each year. But did you know that the pier has a fascinating history that goes back over a century? Originally built in 1909, the Santa Monica Pier was a bustling hub for commercial and recreational fishing. However, it wasn't until the 1920s and 30s that the pier really took off as a popular destination for tourists. During this time, the pier was expanded to include a variety of amusement park rides and games, including a giant Ferris wheel and a roller coaster. One interesting fact about the Santa Monica Pier is that it marks the western end of Route 66, the famous highway that runs from Chicago to Santa Monica. The highway played a significant role in American history, as it provided a vital transportation link between the Midwest and the West Coast. Today, the Santa Monica Pier remains a popular attraction for visitors of all ages.

Santa Monica Pier
200 Santa Monica Pier, Santa Monica, CA 90401

**SCAN QR CODE
TO NAVIGATE**

183

ICONIC PLACE

TOURIST ATTRACTION

CALIFORNIA 1

VENICE BEACH

PACIFIC COAST HWY: 1636 MI/ 2633 KM VENICE, CALIFORNIA
CALIFORNIA HIGHWAY 1: 668 MI/ 1075 KM
33.99325, -118.48059

Greetings from Venice Beach, where the palm trees sway and the ocean waves beckon! Get ready for a fun-filled day in the sun. Venice Beach is a popular beachfront neighborhood located on the west side of Los Angeles, California. It is known for its vibrant boardwalk filled with street performers, artists, vendors, and unique shops. Venice Beach is also famous for Muscle Beach, a popular outdoor gym where many bodybuilders and fitness enthusiasts come to train. Arnold Schwarzenegger, the famous actor and former governor of California, trained at the original Muscle Beach during the 1970s. Another popular attraction is Abbot Kinney Boulevard, a trendy street filled with boutique shops, art galleries, and restaurants. This street was named after Abbot Kinney, the developer who founded Venice Beach in 1905. Venice Beach is also a popular destination for skateboarders from around the world. The boardwalk at Venice is known for its skatepark that attracts many skateboarders and BMX riders.

Venice Beach
Ocean Front Walk, Venice, CA 90291

**SCAN QR CODE
TO NAVIGATE**

184

 OFF THE MAIN ROUTE

 TOURIST ATTRACTION

 ICONIC PLACE

 CALIFORNIA 1

LOS ANGELES DOWNTOWN

DISTANCE FROM STATE ROUTE 1: 20 MI/ 32 KM   LOS ANGELES, CALIFORNIA

34.10147, -118.32672

Welcome to Los Angeles, the entertainment capital of the world! This bustling metropolis, located in Southern California, is famous for its gorgeous beaches, trendy neighborhoods, and thriving arts and culture scene. Let's start with the city's most iconic attraction: the Hollywood Sign. This massive, 45-foot-tall (13,7 meters) sign can be seen from miles away and is a must-see for anyone visiting Los Angeles. You can hike up to the sign for a closer view or snap photos from the Griffith Observatory, which offers stunning panoramic views of the city. Another must-visit attraction is The Hollywood Walk of Fame, which spans 18 blocks along Hollywood Boulevard and features over 2,600 stars honoring celebrities from the entertainment industry. If you're interested in art and culture, be sure to check out the Getty Center, a stunning museum with an extensive collection of European paintings, sculptures, and decorative arts. The museum's architecture and gardens are also worth exploring. At the end, visit Universal Studios Hollywood. To fully appreciate all the attractions downtown Los Angeles has to offer, plan on spending at least three full days.

Hollywood Walk of Fame
Hollywood Boulevard, Vine St, Los Angeles, CA 90028

**SCAN QR CODE
TO NAVIGATE**

TOURIST ATTRACTION

CALIFORNIA

1

AQUARIUM OF THE PACIFIC

PACIFIC COAST HWY: 1664 MI/ 2678 KM LONG BEACH, CALIFORNIA
CALIFORNIA HIGHWAY 1: 696 MI/ 1120 KM
33.76196, -118.19695

While exploring Long Island, why not make a stop at the Aquarium of the Pacific? This well-known California aquarium is definitely worth a visit! As you step inside the aquarium, you'll be transported to an awe-inspiring world of marine life. From the colorful fish and playful sea otters to the majestic sharks and graceful jellyfish, there's something here for everyone to enjoy. One of the most impressive exhibits at the Aquarium of the Pacific is the Tropical Pacific Gallery, which features a stunning array of fish and other sea creatures from the Indo-Pacific region. Here, you'll have the opportunity to witness the beauty and diversity of this vast ocean ecosystem, from the vibrant coral reefs to the elusive seahorses and sea dragons. Another must-see exhibit is the Shark Lagoon, where you'll come face-to-face with some of the ocean's most fearsome predators. Don't worry, though - there's a thick layer of acrylic separating you from the sharks, so you can observe them up close without any danger.

Aquarium of the Pacific
100 Aquarium Way, Long Beach, CA 90802

**SCAN QR CODE
TO NAVIGATE**

186

CALIFORNIA
1

NAPLES CANALS

PACIFIC COAST HWY: 1668 MI/ 2684 KM LONG BEACH, CALIFORNIA
CALIFORNIA HIGHWAY 1: 700 MI/ 1127 KM
33.75278, -118.12411

Naples Canals is a charming neighborhood located in Long Beach. This hidden gem offers visitors a unique and serene experience. The canals were originally built in the 1920s and have been preserved to maintain their historic charm. Take a leisurely stroll along the canals and admire the beautiful homes that line the waterways. The architecture is a mix of Mediterranean and Spanish styles, with many of the homes featuring stunning gardens and water features. The Naples Canals also offer many opportunities for water-based activities such as kayaking and paddleboarding. Several rental companies offer equipment for visitors to explore the canals at their own pace. In addition to the natural beauty of the canals, there are many shops and restaurants. Enjoy a meal or a drink while overlooking the water, or browse the local shops for unique souvenirs and gifts.

Naples Canals Waterway
Naples Canal, Long Beach, CA 90803

**SCAN QR CODE
TO NAVIGATE**

HUNTINGTON BEACH

PACIFIC COAST HWY: 1678 MI/ 2700 KM   HUNTINGTON BEACH, CALIFORNIA
CALIFORNIA HIGHWAY 1: 710 MI/ 1143 KM
33.65597, -118.00337

Welcome to one of the most famous beaches along the entire Pacific Coast Highway. Huntington Beach is an absolute icon, a place of unparalleled natural beauty and wonder. From the crystal clear waters to the pristine white sands, this destination truly has it all. Huntington Beach is an absolute paradise for those who love to watch the sun set over the Pacific. The colors of the sky are nothing short of breathtaking as they melt into the horizon, creating an awe-inspiring display of natural beauty. But that's not all. This beach is also renowned for its fantastic surf conditions, drawing surfers from around the world. With some of the best waves and breaks along the coast, Huntington Beach is the perfect place to catch some gnarly waves or simply watch the pros in action. The beach has a long history of hosting surfing competitions, including the US Open of Surfing, which attracts thousands of spectators every year. So come, step into paradise, and experience the wonder and majesty of Huntington Beach for yourself.

Huntington Beach
351-227 CA-1, Huntington Beach, CA 92648

**SCAN QR CODE
TO NAVIGATE**

HUNTINGTON BEACH
SURFING MUSEUM

PACIFIC COAST HWY: 1678 MI/ 2700 KM HUNTINGTON BEACH, CALIFORNIA
CALIFORNIA HIGHWAY 1: 710 MI/ 1143 KM
33.65916, -118.00076

It's clear that Huntington Beach is a haven for surfers! The Huntington Beach International Surfing Museum, situated near the beach and pier is a must-see attraction for anyone looking to immerse themselves in the local surfing culture. The museum celebrates the history and culture of surfing, featuring exhibits on surfboards, surfers, and the evolution of the sport. Explore the museum's extensive collection of surf memorabilia, including vintage surfboards, photographs, and other artifacts. Adjacent to the museum building, you'll find a small parking lot featuring the World's Largest Surfboard! Additionally, the museum's exterior wall features a stunning surfing mural that makes for a great photo opportunity.

Huntington Beach International Surfing Museum
411 Olive Ave, Huntington Beach, CA 92648

**SCAN QR CODE
TO NAVIGATE**

189

CALIFORNIA 1

BALBOA ISLAND

PACIFIC COAST HWY: 1685 MI/ 2712 KM NEWPORT BEACH, CALIFORNIA
CALIFORNIA HIGHWAY 1: 717 MI/ 1154 KM
33.60630, -117.88968

Make sure to add Balboa Island to your bucket list! This charming man-made island located in Newport Beach, California, is a must-visit destination. A great way to take in the beautiful coastal architecture and scenic views is by renting a bicycle (you can rent a bike at SportsRents LLC) and touring the entire island as well as Balboa Peninsula. As you ride around the island, you'll be able to explore a variety of small shops, galleries, and restaurants, and take in the laid-back coastal vibe that makes this place so special. Don't miss the Balboa Fun Zone, an amusement park with classic rides like a Ferris wheel and bumper cars. Your visit to Balboa Island won't be complete without stopping by the Balboa Island Museum to learn more about the history and culture of this charming island community. The museum is home to a variety of exhibits and artifacts that showcase the area's unique heritage. After exploring the museum, take a break and enjoy a cup of coffee at one of the many cafes. .

Balboa Island Museum
210 Marine Ave, Newport Beach, CA 92662

**SCAN QR CODE
TO NAVIGATE**

INSPIRATION POINT

PACIFIC COAST HWY: 1687 MI/ 2715 KM   CORONA DEL MAR, CALIFORNIA
CALIFORNIA HIGHWAY 1: 719 MI/ 1157 KM
33.59233, -117.87155

As we approach the end of our journey, I invite you to take a moment to reflect on the beauty and wonder you've experienced along the way. Inspiration Point is more than just a breathtaking scenic overlook. It's a reminder of the power of inspiration itself. Traveling is a beautiful thing because it allows us to break free from our routines and experience new places, people, and cultures. It broadens our perspectives and enriches our lives in ways we could never imagine. And Inspiration Point is just one of countless destinations around the world that can inspire us to keep exploring and pushing our boundaries. So as we bid farewell to Inspiration Point, let us carry with us the spirit of inspiration and adventure. Let's continue to seek new experiences and challenge ourselves to see the world in new and exciting ways. Because in the end, it's the journey that matters most, and there's always more to discover.

Inspiration Point
3001 Ocean Blvd, Corona Del Mar, CA 92625

**SCAN QR CODE
TO NAVIGATE**

HISTORICAL LANDMARK

CALIFORNIA

1

PIRATE TOWER

PACIFIC COAST HWY: 1695 MI/ 2728 KM LAGUNA BEACH, CALIFORNIA
CALIFORNIA HIGHWAY 1: 727 MI/ 1170 KM
33.52065, -117.76457

Ahoy matey! Arrr! The Pirate Tower is a unique and intriguing landmark located in Laguna Beach, California. It's a small, castle-like structure that sits on a cliff overlooking the Pacific Ocean. The tower was originally built in the 1920s as a private staircase to provide access to the beach below for a wealthy resident. Over time, the tower took on a mysterious and romantic aura, and many have come to associate it with pirates and buried treasure. The tower is now a popular spot for visitors and locals alike, and is often featured in photographs and artwork depicting the beauty of the California coastline. Arrr!

Pirate Tower
2700 Victoria Dr, Laguna Beach, CA 92651

**SCAN QR CODE
TO NAVIGATE**

OCEAN INSTITUTE

PACIFIC COAST HWY: 1701 MI/ 2737 KM   DANA POINT, CALIFORNIA
CALIFORNIA HIGHWAY 1: 733 MI/ 1180 KM
33.46100, -117.70672

Welcome to Dana Point, the final stop on California's Highway 1! The city is named after Richard Henry Dana Jr., who wrote about the area in his book "Two Years Before the Mast." One of Dana Point's main attractions is the harbor, home to over 2,500 boats and yachts. It's also a popular spot for whale watching tours, sport fishing, and other water activities. While you're here, don't miss the opportunity to visit the Ocean Institute, a world-renowned organization dedicated to marine education, conservation, and research. The institute offers a range of programs and activities, including whale and marine life tours, where you can get up close and personal with some of the ocean's most majestic creatures. Additionally, during the summer months, they organize bioluminescence night cruises, a truly unique and unforgettable experience.

Ocean Institute
24200 Dana Point Harbor Dr, Dana Point, CA 92629

**SCAN QR CODE
TO NAVIGATE**

193

CASA ROMANTICA

PACIFIC COAST HWY: 1707 MI/ 2747 KM SAN CLEMENTE, CALIFORNIA

33.42184, -117.62034

The modern history of San Clemente began in the early 20th century when Ole Hanson, a former mayor of Seattle, purchased the land and developed the city as a planned community. He envisioned San Clemente as a "Spanish Village by the Sea," and the city's architecture reflects this vision to this day. One of the most iconic buildings in San Clemente is the Casa Romantica Cultural Center and Gardens. The building was constructed in 1927 as a private residence for Ole Hanson himself. The house was designed by architect Carl Lindbom and features a blend of Spanish Colonial Revival and Mediterranean Revival styles. Over the years, the Casa Romantica has served as a residence for several families and even as a school before being purchased by the City of San Clemente in 1989. The building underwent extensive renovations and was reopened as a cultural center in 2003. Today, the Casa Romantica is a popular destination for visitors to San Clemente.

Casa Romantica Cultural Center and Gardens
415 Avenida Granada, San Clemente, CA 92672

**SCAN QR CODE
TO NAVIGATE**

OCEANSIDE MUNICIPAL FISHING PIER

PACIFIC COAST HWY: 1729 MI/ 2783 KM OCEANSIDE, CALIFORNIA

33.19339, -117.38598

The city of Oceanside was founded by Andrew Jackson Myers, who settled in the San Luis Rey valley in the late 1870's. The town grew rapidly in the early 20th century, thanks in part to nearby Camp Pendleton, a major Marine Corps base, established during World War II. Today, Oceanside is a popular tourist destination, known for its long sandy beaches, picturesque harbor, and historic pier. Stretching over 1,942 feet (592 meters), the Oceanside Municipal Fishing Pier is one of the longest wooden piers on the West Coast. It was first built in 1888 by a group of local businessmen who wanted to create a place where residents could enjoy the beautiful Pacific Ocean. Over the years, the pier has undergone several renovations, including a complete reconstruction in the 1980s after it was damaged by a storm. Fun fact: In 1937, a group of fishermen caught a 172-pound (78 kg) black sea bass off the pier, setting a record that still stands today.

Oceanside Municipal Fishing Pier
301 The Strand N, Oceanside, CA 92054

SCAN QR CODE TO NAVIGATE

OCEANSIDE MUSEUM OF ART

PACIFIC COAST HWY: 1729 MI/ 2783 KM OCEANSIDE, CALIFORNIA

33.19809, -117.37864

After enjoying some time on the pier and taking a leisurely stroll around Oceanside, I highly recommend immersing yourself in art at the Oceanside Museum of Art. It was founded in 1995 and has since become a prominent cultural institution in the San Diego County region. The museum features a variety of exhibitions throughout the year, showcasing the work of both established and emerging artists. Its permanent collection includes works by artists such as Ken Goldman, James Hubbell, and Jeff Irwin. The Oceanside Museum of Art is situated within two separate buildings, each crafted by prominent Modernist architects hailing from California. The first structure, designed by Irving Gill, boasts a timeless style that complements the more contemporary aesthetic of the adjacent Central Pavilion, crafted by Frederick Fisher. Together, these two buildings form a seamless blend of past and present architectural design.

Oceanside Museum of Art
704 Pier View Wy, Oceanside, CA 92054

**SCAN QR CODE
TO NAVIGATE**

OFF THE MAIN ROUTE

TOURIST ATTRACTION

ICONIC PLACE

PALM SPRINGS

DISTANCE FROM OCEANSIDE: 99 MI/ 159 KM PALM SPRINGS, CALIFORNIA

33.83048, -116.54558

Embark on an unforgettable adventure with the longest detour featured in this travel guide. No PCH journey is truly complete without a visit to stunning Palm Springs, boasting magnificent architecture, picturesque palm-lined streets, and the quintessential sunny California vibe. Palm Springs is a desert resort in California famous for its hot springs, spas, and golf courses. With year-round sunshine and warm temperatures, it's a popular destination for relaxation and outdoor activities. Palm Springs has long been a playground for the rich and famous, and many celebrities have owned homes in the area over the years. Take a ride on the Palm Springs Aerial Tramway for stunning views of Coachella Valley. Explore the art galleries and museums in the Uptown Design District, or soak in the natural hot springs at Desert Hot Springs. You'll need to drive for about two hours from Oceanside to reach Palm Springs, but the journey is definitely worth it. While you're there, consider visiting nearby Joshua Tree National Park.

Palm Springs
Palm Springs, CA 92262

**SCAN QR CODE
TO NAVIGATE**

THE FLOWER FIELDS

PACIFIC COAST HWY: 1735 MI/ 2792 KM CARLSBAD, CALIFORNIA
33.12300, -117.31761

The Flower Fields is a beautiful 50-acre flower farm located in Carlsbad, California. It's famous for its vibrant display of ranunculus flowers which bloom every spring from March to May. The Flower Fields started as a working farm in the early 1920s and the ranunculus bulbs were first planted in the 1930s by Luther Gage, a horticulturist and grower. Over the years, the flower fields became a popular tourist destination, and in 1965, the current owner, Paul Ecke Jr., decided to open up the fields to the public. You can wander through the colorful fields of ranunculus, take tractor rides around the farm, and explore the various gardens, including a rose garden and a sweet pea maze. There are also picnic areas, a playground for children, and a gift shop selling souvenirs and plants.

The Flower Fields
5704 Paseo Del Norte, Carlsbad, CA 92008

**SCAN QR CODE
TO NAVIGATE**

198

CAFE

PANNIKIN COFFEE & TEA

PACIFIC COAST HWY: 1740 MI/ 2800 KM ENCINITAS, CALIFORNIA

33.05830, -117.29964

Encinitas is a coastal city located in San Diego County, California. Its history is closely tied to the arrival of the Santa Fe Railroad in the late 1800s. The railroad played a significant role in the development of Encinitas, providing a means of transportation for both people and goods. If you're looking for a great cup of coffee or tea, you've come to the right place. The Pannikin has been serving the community since 1968 and is a family-owned and operated business that roasts coffee and bakes delicious treats daily. Located in the heart of Encinitas, the Pannikin is a great spot to relax and enjoy a freshly brewed cup of coffee or tea. What's more, the Pannikin is housed in a historic Santa Fe Railroad Station built in 1888. Located on the historic Coast Highway 101, it's a must-visit destination for history buffs and coffee lovers alike.

Pannikin Coffee & Tea
510 N Coast Hwy 101, Encinitas, CA 92024

**SCAN QR CODE
TO NAVIGATE**

SEAWORLD SAN DIEGO

PACIFIC COAST HWY: 1764 MI/ 2839 KM SAN DIEGO, CALIFORNIA
32.76414, -117.22629

Welcome to San Diego! It's the second-largest city in California after Los Angeles. San Diego has a rich history. European settlement began in 1769 and the city became a major port and transportation hub in the 19th century. It next played a key role in the military and defense industries in the 20th century. You can start your exploration of the city at the amazing park, SeaWorld San Diego. This incredible destination promises a world of adventure and entertainment for visitors of all ages. Located on 190 acres of beautiful Mission Bay, this marine mammal park, oceanarium, and theme park is home to a diverse array of marine animals, including whales, dolphins, penguins, sea lions, and sharks. To fully explore the park, I suggest setting aside an entire day due to its vast size.

SeaWorld San Diego
500 Sea World Dr., San Diego, CA 92109

**SCAN QR CODE
TO NAVIGATE**

TO VISIT
VISITED

200

ICONIC PLACE

HISTORICAL LANDMARK

BALBOA PARK

PACIFIC COAST HWY: 1766 MI/ 2842 KM SAN DIEGO, CALIFORNIA
32.73417, -117.14571

Balboa Park is a cultural oasis nestled in the heart of San Diego. This 1,200-acre park is home to numerous gardens, museums, theaters, and recreational spaces. One of the largest urban parks in the United States its history dates back to 1868 when the land was set aside for public use. In 1915, the Panama-California Exposition was held here to celebrate the opening of the Panama Canal. The exposition left behind numerous Spanish colonial-style buildings, including the famous California Tower and the Botanical Building. These buildings are now part of the park's rich cultural heritage and attract thousands of visitors each year. Balboa Park boasts 17 museums, each dedicated to showcasing unique collections and exhibits. Some of the most popular museums include the San Diego Museum of Art, the Museum of Photographic Arts, and the San Diego Natural History Museum. The park also houses the world-renowned San Diego Zoo, home to over 3,500 animals from more than 650 species.

Balboa Park
1549 El Prado, San Diego, CA 92101

**SCAN QR CODE
TO NAVIGATE**

USS MIDWAY MUSEUM

PACIFIC COAST HWY: 1767 MI/ 2844 KM SAN DIEGO, CALIFORNIA

32.71372, -117.17514

San Diego is home to several military bases, including the U.S. Navy's Pacific Fleet. Military enthusiasts simply cannot afford to miss the opportunity to explore the USS Midway Museum. The museum is housed on the USS Midway, a retired Navy aircraft carrier that served from 1945 to 1992. The ship was involved in many historic events, including the Vietnam War and the Gulf War, and is one of the most visited naval ships in the world. One of the most impressive things about the USS Midway is its size. Over 1,000 feet (305 meters) long and 200 feet (61 meters) tall, it weighs more than 69,000 tons. As you explore the ship, you'll get a sense of what life was like for the sailors who served on it. You can visit the sleeping quarters, mess hall, and even the engine room. The USS Midway Museum also features an incredible collection of aircraft. The ship's flight deck is home to more than 30 planes and helicopters, including an F-14 Tomcat, A-6 Intruder, and S-3 Viking. Walk around the flight deck and get up close to these incredible machines.

USS Midway Museum
910 N Harbor Dr, San Diego, CA 92101

**SCAN QR CODE
TO NAVIGATE**

CABRILLO
NATIONAL MONUMENT

PACIFIC COAST HWY: 1775 MI/ 2857 KM SAN DIEGO, CALIFORNIA
32.67202, -117.24138

This is it! This is the last point of our journey! Cabrillo National Monument commemorates the landing of Juan Rodriguez Cabrillo at San Diego Bay on September 28, 1542. This marked the first time a European expedition had set foot on what is now the west coast of the United States. The monument consists of a visitor center, museum, and several hiking trails that offer stunning views of the surrounding landscape and the Pacific Ocean. The centerpiece of the monument is a 14-foot (4,3 meters) tall statue of Juan Rodriguez Cabrillo, which stands on a pedestal overlooking the ocean. Point Loma is also home to the Old Point Loma Lighthouse, which operated from 1855 to 1891 and is now a museum. Congratulations! You've successfully completed the entire Pacific Coast Highway journey from Seattle, Washington, to San Diego, California. Enjoy your time in San Diego, and let the celebration begin!

Cabrillo National Monument
1800 Cabrillo Memorial Dr, San Diego, CA 92106

**SCAN QR CODE
TO NAVIGATE**

CONGRATULATIONS

PACIFIC COAST
HIGHWAY
TRAVELER

....
(Your name, nickname)

This person traveled across Pacific Coast Highway
from .... to ....

Start date...

Finish date..

Total days...

Total places visited...........................

CHECK OUT MY OTHER BOOKS
AVAILABLE FOR SALE ON AMAZON

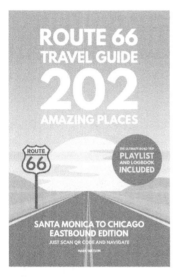

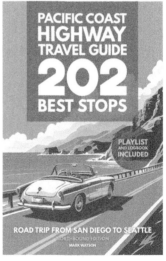

ABOUT THE AUTHOR:

Mark Watson is a member of a Los Angeles Motorcycle Club and an avid traveler based in California. Having ridden his Harley-Davidson along the entire length of the Pacific Coast Highway multiple times, he knows the road like the back of his hand. He is also a bestselling author on Amazon, with two other popular travel guides: "Route 66 Travel Guide - 202 Amazing Places" and "Alaska Highway Travel Guide - 202 Best Stops."

PLEASE RATE THIS BOOK AND ADD A REVIEW IF YOU ENJOYED IT. THIS WILL REWARD ALL THE HARD WORK PUT INTO THIS TRAVEL GUIDE AND HELP OTHERS ALL OVER THE WORLD START THEIR OWN JOURNEY ON THE PACIFIC COAST HIGHWAY.

DON'T FORGET TO ADD HASHTAG #202PCH
IF YOU SHARE PHOTOS OR VIDEOS ON SOCIAL MEDIA.

FOR BUSINESS AND PRIVATE INQUIRIES,
PLEASE CONTACT:

MARKWATSONTRAVELER@GMAIL.COM

MARKWATSON.TRAVELER

WWW.MARKWATSONTRAVELER.COM

PACIFIC COAST HWY

PACIFIC COAST HIGHWAY
TRAVEL JOURNAL
LOGBOOK

DAY NUMBER.......... DATE..................

STARTING POINT: .... MILEAGE ☐☐☐☐

ENDING POINT: .... MILEAGE ☐☐☐☐

WHERE I STAYED FOR THE NIGHT/RV PARK:

....

WEATHER:

☐ ☐ ☐

☐ ☐ ☐

TEMPERATURE: ....

PEOPLE I MET: ....

....

....

THINGS I WILL REMEMBER:

....

....

....

PLACES THAT I VISITED:

WRITE THE PLACE NUMBERS
FOR EACH LOCATION VISITED

◯ ◯ ◯ ◯

◯ ◯ ◯ ◯

◯ ◯ ◯ ◯

◯ ◯ ◯ ◯

◯ ◯ ◯ ◯

◯ ◯ ◯ ◯

ADDITIONAL PLACES THAT I SAW:

....

....

....

....

DAY NUMBER............ DATE...................

STARTING POINT: .... MILEAGE ☐☐☐☐

ENDING POINT: .... MILEAGE ☐☐☐☐

WHERE I STAYED FOR THE NIGHT/RV PARK:

....

WEATHER:

☐ ☐ ☐

☐ ☐ ☐

🌡 TEMPERATURE: ....

👤 PEOPLE I MET: ....

....

....

THINGS I WILL REMEMBER:

....

....

....

PLACES THAT I VISITED:
WRITE THE PLACE NUMBERS
FOR EACH LOCATION VISITED

◯ ◯ ◯ ◯

◯ ◯ ◯ ◯

◯ ◯ ◯ ◯

◯ ◯ ◯ ◯

◯ ◯ ◯ ◯

◯ ◯ ◯ ◯

ADDITIONAL PLACES THAT I SAW:

....

....

....

....

DAY NUMBER .... DATE ....

STARTING POINT: .... MILEAGE ☐☐☐☐

ENDING POINT: .... MILEAGE ☐☐☐☐

WHERE I STAYED FOR THE NIGHT/RV PARK:

....

WEATHER:

☐ ☐ ☐

☐ ☐ ☐

🌡 TEMPERATURE: ....

👤 PEOPLE I MET: ....

....

....

THINGS I WILL REMEMBER:

....

....

....

PLACES THAT I VISITED:

WRITE THE PLACE NUMBERS
FOR EACH LOCATION VISITED

◯ ◯ ◯ ◯

◯ ◯ ◯ ◯

◯ ◯ ◯ ◯

◯ ◯ ◯ ◯

◯ ◯ ◯ ◯

◯ ◯ ◯ ◯

ADDITIONAL PLACES THAT I SAW:

....

....

....

....

DAY NUMBER.......... DATE..........

STARTING POINT: .... MILEAGE ☐☐☐☐

ENDING POINT: .... MILEAGE ☐☐☐☐

WHERE I STAYED FOR THE NIGHT/RV PARK:

....

WEATHER:

☐ ☐ ☐

☐ ☐ ☐

🌡 TEMPERATURE: ....

🧍 PEOPLE I MET: ....

....

....

THINGS I WILL REMEMBER:

....

....

....

PLACES THAT I VISITED:

WRITE THE PLACE NUMBERS
FOR EACH LOCATION VISITED

◯ ◯ ◯ ◯

◯ ◯ ◯ ◯

◯ ◯ ◯ ◯

◯ ◯ ◯ ◯

◯ ◯ ◯ ◯

◯ ◯ ◯ ◯

ADDITIONAL PLACES THAT I SAW:

....

....

....

....

DAY NUMBER......... DATE.............

STARTING POINT: .... MILEAGE ☐☐☐☐

ENDING POINT: .... MILEAGE ☐☐☐☐

WHERE I STAYED FOR THE NIGHT/RV PARK:

....

WEATHER:

☐   ☐   ☐

☐   ☐   ☐

🌡 TEMPERATURE: ....

👤 PEOPLE I MET: ....

....

....

THINGS I WILL REMEMBER:

....

....

....

PLACES THAT I VISITED:

WRITE THE PLACE NUMBERS
FOR EACH LOCATION VISITED

◯ ◯ ◯ ◯

◯ ◯ ◯ ◯

◯ ◯ ◯ ◯

◯ ◯ ◯ ◯

◯ ◯ ◯ ◯

◯ ◯ ◯ ◯

ADDITIONAL PLACES THAT I SAW:

....

....

....

....

DAY NUMBER .... DATE ....

STARTING POINT: .... MILEAGE ☐☐☐☐

ENDING POINT: .... MILEAGE ☐☐☐☐

WHERE I STAYED FOR THE NIGHT/RV PARK:

....

WEATHER:

☐ ☐ ☐

☐ ☐ ☐

🌡 TEMPERATURE: ....

👤 PEOPLE I MET: ....

....

....

THINGS I WILL REMEMBER:

....

....

....

PLACES THAT I VISITED:

WRITE THE PLACE NUMBERS
FOR EACH LOCATION VISITED

◯ ◯ ◯ ◯

◯ ◯ ◯ ◯

◯ ◯ ◯ ◯

◯ ◯ ◯ ◯

◯ ◯ ◯ ◯

◯ ◯ ◯ ◯

ADDITIONAL PLACES THAT I SAW:

....

....

....

....

DAY NUMBER .... DATE ....

STARTING POINT: .... MILEAGE ☐☐☐☐

ENDING POINT: .... MILEAGE ☐☐☐☐

WHERE I STAYED FOR THE NIGHT/RV PARK:

....

WEATHER:

☐ ☐ ☐

☐ ☐ ☐

🌡 TEMPERATURE: ....

👤 PEOPLE I MET: ....

....

....

THINGS I WILL REMEMBER:

....

....

....

PLACES THAT I VISITED:

WRITE THE PLACE NUMBERS
FOR EACH LOCATION VISITED

◯ ◯ ◯ ◯

◯ ◯ ◯ ◯

◯ ◯ ◯ ◯

◯ ◯ ◯ ◯

◯ ◯ ◯ ◯

◯ ◯ ◯ ◯

ADDITIONAL PLACES THAT I SAW:

....

....

....

DAY NUMBER .... DATE ....

STARTING POINT: .... MILEAGE ☐☐☐☐

ENDING POINT: .... MILEAGE ☐☐☐☐

WHERE I STAYED FOR THE NIGHT/RV PARK:

....

WEATHER:

☐   ☐   ☐

☐   ☐   ☐

🌡 TEMPERATURE: ....

👤 PEOPLE I MET: ....

....

....

THINGS I WILL REMEMBER:

....

....

....

PLACES THAT I VISITED:

WRITE THE PLACE NUMBERS
FOR EACH LOCATION VISITED

◯ ◯ ◯ ◯

◯ ◯ ◯ ◯

◯ ◯ ◯ ◯

◯ ◯ ◯ ◯

◯ ◯ ◯ ◯

◯ ◯ ◯ ◯

ADDITIONAL PLACES THAT I SAW:

....

....

....

....

DAY NUMBER......... DATE.........

STARTING POINT: .... MILEAGE ☐☐☐☐

ENDING POINT: .... MILEAGE ☐☐☐☐

WHERE I STAYED FOR THE NIGHT/RV PARK:

....

WEATHER:

☐   ☐   ☐

☐   ☐   ☐

🌡 TEMPERATURE: ....

👤 PEOPLE I MET: ....

....

....

THINGS I WILL REMEMBER:

....

....

....

PLACES THAT I VISITED:

WRITE THE PLACE NUMBERS
FOR EACH LOCATION VISITED

◯ ◯ ◯ ◯

◯ ◯ ◯ ◯

◯ ◯ ◯ ◯

◯ ◯ ◯ ◯

◯ ◯ ◯ ◯

◯ ◯ ◯ ◯

ADDITIONAL PLACES THAT I SAW:

....

....

....

....

DAY NUMBER........ DATE........

STARTING POINT:........................ MILEAGE ☐☐☐☐

ENDING POINT:........................ MILEAGE ☐☐☐☐

WHERE I STAYED FOR THE NIGHT/RV PARK:

....

WEATHER:

☐ ☐ ☐

☐ ☐ ☐

🌡 TEMPERATURE:...........

👤 PEOPLE I MET:...........

....

....

THINGS I WILL REMEMBER:

....

....

....

PLACES THAT I VISITED:
WRITE THE PLACE NUMBERS
FOR EACH LOCATION VISITED

○ ○ ○ ○

○ ○ ○ ○

○ ○ ○ ○

○ ○ ○ ○

○ ○ ○ ○

○ ○ ○ ○

ADDITIONAL PLACES THAT I SAW:

....

....

....

....

DAY NUMBER .... DATE ....

STARTING POINT: .... MILEAGE ☐☐☐☐

ENDING POINT: .... MILEAGE ☐☐☐☐

WHERE I STAYED FOR THE NIGHT/RV PARK:

....

WEATHER:

☐   ☐   ☐

☐   ☐   ☐

🌡 TEMPERATURE: ....

👤 PEOPLE I MET: ....

....

....

THINGS I WILL REMEMBER:

....

....

....

PLACES THAT I VISITED:

WRITE THE PLACE NUMBERS
FOR EACH LOCATION VISITED

◯ ◯ ◯ ◯

◯ ◯ ◯ ◯

◯ ◯ ◯ ◯

◯ ◯ ◯ ◯

◯ ◯ ◯ ◯

◯ ◯ ◯ ◯

ADDITIONAL PLACES THAT I SAW:

....

....

....

....

DAY NUMBER......... DATE.................

STARTING POINT:............................ MILEAGE ☐☐☐☐

ENDING POINT:............................. MILEAGE ☐☐☐☐

WHERE I STAYED FOR THE NIGHT/RV PARK:

....

WEATHER:

☀ ☐   ☁ ☐   ⛅ ☐

❄ ☐   🌧 ☐   ⛈ ☐

🌡 TEMPERATURE: ....

👤 PEOPLE I MET: ....

....

....

THINGS I WILL REMEMBER:

....

....

....

PLACES THAT I VISITED:

WRITE THE PLACE NUMBERS
FOR EACH LOCATION VISITED

◯ ◯ ◯ ◯

◯ ◯ ◯ ◯

◯ ◯ ◯ ◯

◯ ◯ ◯ ◯

◯ ◯ ◯ ◯

◯ ◯ ◯ ◯

ADDITIONAL PLACES THAT I SAW:

....

....

....

....

DAY NUMBER .... DATE ....

STARTING POINT: .... MILEAGE ☐☐☐☐

ENDING POINT: .... MILEAGE ☐☐☐☐

WHERE I STAYED FOR THE NIGHT/RV PARK:

....

WEATHER:

☐ ☐ ☐

☐ ☐ ☐

🌡 TEMPERATURE: ....

👤 PEOPLE I MET: ....

....

....

THINGS I WILL REMEMBER:

....

....

....

PLACES THAT I VISITED:

WRITE THE PLACE NUMBERS
FOR EACH LOCATION VISITED

◯ ◯ ◯ ◯

◯ ◯ ◯ ◯

◯ ◯ ◯ ◯

◯ ◯ ◯ ◯

◯ ◯ ◯ ◯

◯ ◯ ◯ ◯

ADDITIONAL PLACES THAT I SAW:

....

....

....

....

DAY NUMBER .... DATE ....

STARTING POINT: .... MILEAGE ☐☐☐☐

ENDING POINT: .... MILEAGE ☐☐☐☐

WHERE I STAYED FOR THE NIGHT/RV PARK:

....

WEATHER:

☐ ☐ ☐

☐ ☐ ☐

🌡 TEMPERATURE: ....

👤 PEOPLE I MET: ....

....

....

THINGS I WILL REMEMBER:

....

....

....

PLACES THAT I VISITED:
WRITE THE PLACE NUMBERS
FOR EACH LOCATION VISITED

○ ○ ○ ○

○ ○ ○ ○

○ ○ ○ ○

○ ○ ○ ○

○ ○ ○ ○

○ ○ ○ ○

ADDITIONAL PLACES THAT I SAW:

....

....

....

....

DAY NUMBER .... DATE ....

STARTING POINT: .... MILEAGE ☐☐☐☐

ENDING POINT: .... MILEAGE ☐☐☐☐

WHERE I STAYED FOR THE NIGHT/RV PARK:

....

WEATHER:

☀ ☐   ☁ ☐   ⛅ ☐

❄ ☐   🌧 ☐   ⛈ ☐

🌡 TEMPERATURE: ....

👤 PEOPLE I MET: ....

....

....

THINGS I WILL REMEMBER:

....

....

....

PLACES THAT I VISITED:

WRITE THE PLACE NUMBERS
FOR EACH LOCATION VISITED

◯ ◯ ◯ ◯

◯ ◯ ◯ ◯

◯ ◯ ◯ ◯

◯ ◯ ◯ ◯

◯ ◯ ◯ ◯

◯ ◯ ◯ ◯

ADDITIONAL PLACES THAT I SAW:

....

....

....

....

DAY NUMBER......... DATE.................

STARTING POINT:............................. MILEAGE ☐☐☐☐

ENDING POINT:............................. MILEAGE ☐☐☐☐

WHERE I STAYED FOR THE NIGHT/RV PARK:

....

WEATHER:

☐ ☐ ☐

☐ ☐ ☐

🌡 TEMPERATURE: ....

👤 PEOPLE I MET: ....

....

....

THINGS I WILL REMEMBER:

....

....

....

PLACES THAT I VISITED:

WRITE THE PLACE NUMBERS
FOR EACH LOCATION VISITED

◯ ◯ ◯ ◯

◯ ◯ ◯ ◯

◯ ◯ ◯ ◯

◯ ◯ ◯ ◯

◯ ◯ ◯ ◯

◯ ◯ ◯ ◯

ADDITIONAL PLACES THAT I SAW:

....

....

....

....

DAY NUMBER .... DATE ....

STARTING POINT: .... MILEAGE ☐☐☐☐

ENDING POINT: .... MILEAGE ☐☐☐☐

WHERE I STAYED FOR THE NIGHT/RV PARK:

....

WEATHER:

☀ ☐   ☁ ☐   ⛅ ☐

❄ ☐   🌧 ☐   ⛈ ☐

🌡 TEMPERATURE: ....

👤 PEOPLE I MET: ....

....

....

THINGS I WILL REMEMBER:

....

....

....

PLACES THAT I VISITED:

WRITE THE PLACE NUMBERS
FOR EACH LOCATION VISITED

◯ ◯ ◯ ◯

◯ ◯ ◯ ◯

◯ ◯ ◯ ◯

◯ ◯ ◯ ◯

◯ ◯ ◯ ◯

◯ ◯ ◯ ◯

ADDITIONAL PLACES THAT I SAW:

....

....

....

....

DAY NUMBER............ DATE....................

STARTING POINT:............................... MILEAGE ☐☐☐☐

ENDING POINT:............................... MILEAGE ☐☐☐☐

WHERE I STAYED FOR THE NIGHT/RV PARK:

....

WEATHER:

☐   ☐   ☐

☐   ☐   ☐

🌡 TEMPERATURE:...............

👤 PEOPLE I MET:...............

....

....

THINGS I WILL REMEMBER:

....

....

....

PLACES THAT I VISITED:

WRITE THE PLACE NUMBERS
FOR EACH LOCATION VISITED

◯ ◯ ◯ ◯

◯ ◯ ◯ ◯

◯ ◯ ◯ ◯

◯ ◯ ◯ ◯

◯ ◯ ◯ ◯

◯ ◯ ◯ ◯

ADDITIONAL PLACES THAT I SAW:

....

....

....

....

DAY NUMBER......... DATE.........

STARTING POINT: .... MILEAGE ☐☐☐☐

ENDING POINT: .... MILEAGE ☐☐☐☐

WHERE I STAYED FOR THE NIGHT/RV PARK:

....

WEATHER:

☐ ☐ ☐

☐ ☐ ☐

🌡 TEMPERATURE: ....

👤 PEOPLE I MET: ....

....

....

THINGS I WILL REMEMBER:

....

....

....

PLACES THAT I VISITED:

WRITE THE PLACE NUMBERS
FOR EACH LOCATION VISITED

◯ ◯ ◯ ◯

◯ ◯ ◯ ◯

◯ ◯ ◯ ◯

◯ ◯ ◯ ◯

◯ ◯ ◯ ◯

◯ ◯ ◯ ◯

ADDITIONAL PLACES THAT I SAW:

....

....

....

....

DAY NUMBER .... DATE ....

STARTING POINT: .... MILEAGE ☐☐☐☐

ENDING POINT: .... MILEAGE ☐☐☐☐

WHERE I STAYED FOR THE NIGHT/RV PARK:

....

WEATHER:

☀ ☐   ☁ ☐   ⛅ ☐

❄ ☐   🌧 ☐   ⛈ ☐

🌡 TEMPERATURE: ....

👤 PEOPLE I MET: ....

....

....

THINGS I WILL REMEMBER:

....

....

....

PLACES THAT I VISITED:

WRITE THE PLACE NUMBERS
FOR EACH LOCATION VISITED

◯ ◯ ◯ ◯

◯ ◯ ◯ ◯

◯ ◯ ◯ ◯

◯ ◯ ◯ ◯

◯ ◯ ◯ ◯

◯ ◯ ◯ ◯

ADDITIONAL PLACES THAT I SAW:

....

....

....

....

DAY NUMBER .... DATE ....

STARTING POINT: .... MILEAGE ☐☐☐☐

ENDING POINT: .... MILEAGE ☐☐☐☐

WHERE I STAYED FOR THE NIGHT/RV PARK:

....

WEATHER:

☐ ☐ ☐

☐ ☐ ☐

🌡 TEMPERATURE: ....

👤 PEOPLE I MET: ....

....

....

THINGS I WILL REMEMBER:

....

....

....

PLACES THAT I VISITED:

WRITE THE PLACE NUMBERS
FOR EACH LOCATION VISITED

◯ ◯ ◯ ◯

◯ ◯ ◯ ◯

◯ ◯ ◯ ◯

◯ ◯ ◯ ◯

◯ ◯ ◯ ◯

◯ ◯ ◯ ◯

ADDITIONAL PLACES THAT I SAW:

....

....

....

DAY NUMBER .... DATE ....

STARTING POINT: .... MILEAGE ☐☐☐☐

ENDING POINT: .... MILEAGE ☐☐☐☐

WHERE I STAYED FOR THE NIGHT/RV PARK:

....

WEATHER:

☐ ☐ ☐

☐ ☐ ☐

🌡 TEMPERATURE: ....

🧍 PEOPLE I MET: ....

....

....

THINGS I WILL REMEMBER:

....

....

....

PLACES THAT I VISITED:

WRITE THE PLACE NUMBERS
FOR EACH LOCATION VISITED

○ ○ ○ ○

○ ○ ○ ○

○ ○ ○ ○

○ ○ ○ ○

○ ○ ○ ○

○ ○ ○ ○

ADDITIONAL PLACES THAT I SAW:

....

....

....

....

DAY NUMBER .... DATE ....

STARTING POINT: .... MILEAGE ☐☐☐☐

ENDING POINT: .... MILEAGE ☐☐☐☐

WHERE I STAYED FOR THE NIGHT/RV PARK:

....

WEATHER:

☐ ☐ ☐

☐ ☐ ☐

🌡 TEMPERATURE: ....

👤 PEOPLE I MET: ....

....

....

THINGS I WILL REMEMBER:

....

....

....

PLACES THAT I VISITED:

WRITE THE PLACE NUMBERS
FOR EACH LOCATION VISITED

◯ ◯ ◯ ◯

◯ ◯ ◯ ◯

◯ ◯ ◯ ◯

◯ ◯ ◯ ◯

◯ ◯ ◯ ◯

◯ ◯ ◯ ◯

ADDITIONAL PLACES THAT I SAW:

....

....

....

....

DAY NUMBER......... DATE.........

STARTING POINT: .... MILEAGE ☐☐☐☐

ENDING POINT: .... MILEAGE ☐☐☐☐

WHERE I STAYED FOR THE NIGHT/RV PARK:

....

WEATHER:

☐ ☐ ☐

☐ ☐ ☐

🌡 TEMPERATURE: ....

👤 PEOPLE I MET: ....

....

....

THINGS I WILL REMEMBER:

....

....

....

PLACES THAT I VISITED:
WRITE THE PLACE NUMBERS
FOR EACH LOCATION VISITED

◯ ◯ ◯ ◯

◯ ◯ ◯ ◯

◯ ◯ ◯ ◯

◯ ◯ ◯ ◯

◯ ◯ ◯ ◯

◯ ◯ ◯ ◯

ADDITIONAL PLACES THAT I SAW:

....

....

....

....

DAY NUMBER .... DATE ....

STARTING POINT: .... MILEAGE ☐☐☐☐

ENDING POINT: .... MILEAGE ☐☐☐☐

WHERE I STAYED FOR THE NIGHT/RV PARK:

....

WEATHER:

☐ ☐ ☐

☐ ☐ ☐

🌡 TEMPERATURE: ....

👤 PEOPLE I MET: ....

....

....

THINGS I WILL REMEMBER:

....

....

....

PLACES THAT I VISITED:

WRITE THE PLACE NUMBERS
FOR EACH LOCATION VISITED

◯ ◯ ◯ ◯

◯ ◯ ◯ ◯

◯ ◯ ◯ ◯

◯ ◯ ◯ ◯

◯ ◯ ◯ ◯

◯ ◯ ◯ ◯

ADDITIONAL PLACES THAT I SAW:

....

....

....

....

DAY NUMBER......... DATE..................

STARTING POINT:........................... MILEAGE ☐☐☐☐

ENDING POINT:............................. MILEAGE ☐☐☐☐

WHERE I STAYED FOR THE NIGHT/RV PARK:

....

WEATHER:

☐ ☐ ☐

☐ ☐ ☐

🌡 TEMPERATURE: ....

👤 PEOPLE I MET: ....

....

....

THINGS I WILL REMEMBER:

....

....

....

PLACES THAT I VISITED:

WRITE THE PLACE NUMBERS
FOR EACH LOCATION VISITED

◯ ◯ ◯ ◯

◯ ◯ ◯ ◯

◯ ◯ ◯ ◯

◯ ◯ ◯ ◯

◯ ◯ ◯ ◯

◯ ◯ ◯ ◯

ADDITIONAL PLACES THAT I SAW:

....

....

....

....

DAY NUMBER .... DATE ....

STARTING POINT: .... MILEAGE ☐☐☐☐

ENDING POINT: .... MILEAGE ☐☐☐☐

WHERE I STAYED FOR THE NIGHT/RV PARK:

....

WEATHER:

☐ ☐ ☐

☐ ☐ ☐

🌡 TEMPERATURE: ....

👤 PEOPLE I MET: ....

....

....

THINGS I WILL REMEMBER:

....

....

....

PLACES THAT I VISITED:

WRITE THE PLACE NUMBERS
FOR EACH LOCATION VISITED

◯ ◯ ◯ ◯

◯ ◯ ◯ ◯

◯ ◯ ◯ ◯

◯ ◯ ◯ ◯

◯ ◯ ◯ ◯

◯ ◯ ◯ ◯

ADDITIONAL PLACES THAT I SAW:

....

....

....

....

DAY NUMBER............ DATE....................

STARTING POINT:............................... MILEAGE ☐☐☐☐

ENDING POINT:............................... MILEAGE ☐☐☐☐

WHERE I STAYED FOR THE NIGHT/RV PARK:

....

WEATHER:

☐ ☐ ☐

☐ ☐ ☐

🌡 TEMPERATURE: ....

👤 PEOPLE I MET: ....

....

....

THINGS I WILL REMEMBER:

....

....

....

PLACES THAT I VISITED:

WRITE THE PLACE NUMBERS
FOR EACH LOCATION VISITED

◯ ◯ ◯ ◯

◯ ◯ ◯ ◯

◯ ◯ ◯ ◯

◯ ◯ ◯ ◯

◯ ◯ ◯ ◯

◯ ◯ ◯ ◯

ADDITIONAL PLACES THAT I SAW:

....

....

....

DAY NUMBER .... DATE ....

STARTING POINT: .... MILEAGE ☐☐☐☐

ENDING POINT: .... MILEAGE ☐☐☐☐

WHERE I STAYED FOR THE NIGHT/RV PARK:

....

WEATHER:

☀ ☐   ☁ ☐   ⛅ ☐

❄ ☐   🌧 ☐   ⛈ ☐

🌡 TEMPERATURE: ....

👤 PEOPLE I MET: ....

....

....

THINGS I WILL REMEMBER:

....

....

....

PLACES THAT I VISITED:

WRITE THE PLACE NUMBERS
FOR EACH LOCATION VISITED

◯ ◯ ◯ ◯

◯ ◯ ◯ ◯

◯ ◯ ◯ ◯

◯ ◯ ◯ ◯

◯ ◯ ◯ ◯

◯ ◯ ◯ ◯

ADDITIONAL PLACES THAT I SAW:

....

....

....

....

DAY NUMBER .... DATE ....

STARTING POINT: .... MILEAGE ☐☐☐☐

ENDING POINT: .... MILEAGE ☐☐☐☐

WHERE I STAYED FOR THE NIGHT/RV PARK:

....

WEATHER:

☐   ☐   ☐

☐   ☐   ☐

TEMPERATURE: ....

PEOPLE I MET: ....

....

....

THINGS I WILL REMEMBER:

....

....

....

PLACES THAT I VISITED:

WRITE THE PLACE NUMBERS
FOR EACH LOCATION VISITED

◯ ◯ ◯ ◯

◯ ◯ ◯ ◯

◯ ◯ ◯ ◯

◯ ◯ ◯ ◯

◯ ◯ ◯ ◯

◯ ◯ ◯ ◯

ADDITIONAL PLACES THAT I SAW:

....

....

....

....

DAY NUMBER .... DATE ....

STARTING POINT: .... MILEAGE ☐☐☐☐

ENDING POINT: .... MILEAGE ☐☐☐☐

WHERE I STAYED FOR THE NIGHT/RV PARK:

....

WEATHER:

☐   ☐   ☐

☐   ☐   ☐

TEMPERATURE: ....

PEOPLE I MET: ....

....

....

THINGS I WILL REMEMBER:

....

....

....

PLACES THAT I VISITED:

WRITE THE PLACE NUMBERS
FOR EACH LOCATION VISITED

◯ ◯ ◯ ◯

◯ ◯ ◯ ◯

◯ ◯ ◯ ◯

◯ ◯ ◯ ◯

◯ ◯ ◯ ◯

◯ ◯ ◯ ◯

ADDITIONAL PLACES THAT I SAW:

....

....

....

....

DAY NUMBER............ DATE....................

STARTING POINT: .... MILEAGE ☐☐☐☐

ENDING POINT: .... MILEAGE ☐☐☐☐

WHERE I STAYED FOR THE NIGHT/RV PARK:

....

WEATHER:

☐ ☐ ☐

☐ ☐ ☐

🌡 TEMPERATURE: ....

🧍 PEOPLE I MET: ....

....

....

THINGS I WILL REMEMBER:

....

....

....

PLACES THAT I VISITED:

WRITE THE PLACE NUMBERS
FOR EACH LOCATION VISITED

◯ ◯ ◯ ◯

◯ ◯ ◯ ◯

◯ ◯ ◯ ◯

◯ ◯ ◯ ◯

◯ ◯ ◯ ◯

◯ ◯ ◯ ◯

ADDITIONAL PLACES THAT I SAW:

....

....

....

....

NOTES

NOTES

NOTES

NOTES

AUTHOR: MARK WATSON
GRAPHIC DESIGN AND CONCEPT: BART TROCH
EDITOR: RUSS L.
COPYRIGHT 2023
LOS ANGELES, CA, U.S.A.

42859493R00177